KW-221-105

OFFICIAL SQA PAST PAPERS WITH ANSWERS

**INTERMEDIATE 2**

# PHYSICAL EDUCATION
## 2008-2012

© Scottish Qualifications Authority

All rights reserved. Copying prohibited. No part of this publication may be reproduced, stored in a retrieval system, or transmitted in any form or by any means, electronic, mechanical, photocopying, recording or otherwise.

First exam published in 2008.

Published by Bright Red Publishing Ltd, 6 Stafford Street, Edinburgh EH3 7AU

tel: 0131 220 5804 fax: 0131 220 6710 info@brightredpublishing.co.uk  www.brightredpublishing.co.uk

ISBN 978-1-84948-278-3

A CIP Catalogue record for this book is available from the British Library.

Bright Red Publishing is grateful to the copyright holders, as credited on the final page of the Question Section, for permission to use their material. Every effort has been made to trace the copyright holders and to obtain their permission for the use of copyright material. Bright Red Publishing will be happy to receive information allowing us to rectify any error or omission in future editions.

# 2008

[BLANK PAGE]

# X205/201

NATIONAL
QUALIFICATIONS
2008

WEDNESDAY, 28 MAY
1.00 PM – 3.00 PM

PHYSICAL
EDUCATION
INTERMEDIATE 2

Candidates should attempt **THREE** questions, each chosen from a different section.

**SECTION 1—PERFORMANCE APPRECIATION**

*Marks*

## QUESTION 1

Choose **one** activity.

(a) **Technical    Physical    Personal    Special**

From the list of performance qualities above, outline the **range** of qualities you would expect a model performer to demonstrate in your chosen activity.    **5**

(b) Explain how the use of an appropriate model performance helps you develop a personal improvement plan.    **4**

(c) Choose **one** of the qualities listed in Part (a). Describe **one** weakness in your performance with reference to the chosen quality.    **4**

(d) Give examples of the short and long term goals you set yourself to improve your weakness.    **4**

(e) Describe, briefly, the methods you used to monitor your short and long term goals.    **3**

**(20)**

## QUESTION 2

Choose **one** activity.

(a) Describe the challenges you faced in this activity.    **4**

(b) Choose **two** of the qualities from the list below and explain how **each** affected your performance.

- Technical (refinement, timing, effectiveness)
- Physical (strong, light)
- Personal (determination)
- Special (imagination, flair)    **5**

(c) Describe the training you carried out to improve your performance.    **4**

(d) How can mental factors affect your training? Give specific examples.    **4**

(e) What effects did your training have on your performance?    **3**

**(20)**

## SECTION 2—PREPARATION OF THE BODY

*Marks*

### QUESTION 3

Choose **one** activity.

(a)  **Physical fitness      Skill-related fitness      Mental fitness**

How does **each** of the above types of fitness affect performance in your chosen activity?    5

(b)  Select **one** of the types listed in Part (a).  Select **one** aspect of fitness from this type.  Describe how you assessed your level of fitness for the aspect selected.    4

(c)  Why is it important to gather information on your specific fitness needs before planning a training programme?    3

(d)  Describe your specific fitness needs.  Give examples.    3

(e)  What course of action did you take to meet your specific fitness needs?    5

    (20)

### QUESTION 4

Choose **one** activity.

(a)  Select an aspect of fitness.  Describe in detail a training programme to develop this aspect of fitness.    5

(b)  How did you apply the principles of training to your training programme?    5

(c)  How did you monitor the effectiveness of your training programme?    3

(d)  Why was it important to monitor your training programme?    3

(e)  Describe the effect your training had on your performance.    4

    (20)

**[Turn over**

## SECTION 3—SKILLS AND TECHNIQUES

*Marks*

### QUESTION 5

Choose **one** activity.

(*a*)   With reference to the list below, describe what makes a skilled performance.

- Fluency
- Controlled movement
- Decision making
- Appropriate skills and technique                                                        **5**

(*b*)   Describe **your** performance in relation to the skilled performance in Part (*a*).   **4**

(*c*)   Describe how you planned a programme of improvement.                                 **4**

(*d*)   How did the improvement programme help your **whole** performance?                   **4**

(*e*)   What would you now regard as your development needs to further improve
        **your** performance?                                                               **3**

                                                                                         **(20)**

### QUESTION 6

Choose **one** activity.

(*a*)   Describe **one** skill or technique that you regard as a weakness in your
        performance.                                                                         **4**

(*b*)   Describe the methods you used to analyse the weakness identified in Part (*a*).       **4**

(*c*)   Describe **two** methods of practice you used to develop the skill or technique
        you identified as a weakness in Part (*a*).                                          **4**

(*d*)   Explain why these **two** methods helped to improve the weakness in your skill
        or technique.                                                                        **4**

(*e*)   Choose **one** of the following factors.

- Motivation
- Concentration
- Feedback

Explain the importance of this factor in your performance.                                  **4**

                                                                                         **(20)**

## SECTION 4—STRUCTURES, STRATEGIES AND COMPOSITION

*Marks*

### QUESTION 7

Choose **one** activity.

(a) Select a structure, strategy or composition. Explain why it was important to gather information on that structure, strategy or composition. **4**

(b) Describe **one** method you used to gather information about your performance within the structure, strategy or composition. **4**

(c) Explain how your strengths and weaknesses affected the structure, strategy or composition. **5**

(d) What actions did you take to improve the effectiveness of your performance? **4**

(e) Explain the effects your actions had on your performance. **3**

**(20)**

### QUESTION 8

Choose **one** activity.

(a) Describe in **detail** one structure, strategy or composition you have used. **4**

(b) Describe the programme of work you went through to learn this structure, strategy or composition. **4**

(c) Choose **one** of the factors below.

- Use of space in performance
- Use of repetition in performance
- Use of creativity in performance
- Use of width/depth/mobility
- Use of motifs in performance
- Use of speed/tempo in performance

Explain the importance of this factor in your chosen structure, strategy or composition. **4**

(d) Why is continually monitoring your structure, strategy or composition important? **4**

(e) To improve your structure, strategy or composition further, what do you see as your future development needs? **4**

**(20)**

*[END OF QUESTION PAPER]*

[BLANK PAGE]

# INTERMEDIATE 2

# 2009

[BLANK PAGE]

# X205/201

NATIONAL
QUALIFICATIONS
2009

MONDAY, 1 JUNE
1.00 PM – 3.00 PM

PHYSICAL
EDUCATION
INTERMEDIATE 2

Candidates should attempt **THREE** questions, each chosen from a different section.

## SECTION 1—PERFORMANCE APPRECIATION

*Marks*

## QUESTION 1

Choose **one** activity.

(a)    Describe, in detail, a quality performance in this activity.    5

(b)    Outline a goal you set to achieve your own quality performance.    3

(c)    Describe the improvement programme you used to achieve your goal.    4

(d)    Choose **two** factors from the list below.

| | | |
|---|---|---|
| **Confidence** | **Concentration** | **Motivation** |
| **Determination** | **Aggression** | **Stress** |

Explain how these factors affected your whole performance.    4

(e)    Choose **one** or **more** of the method(s) from the list below.

| | |
|---|---|
| **Imagery/Visualisation** | **Deep Breathing** |
| **Relaxation Techniques** | **Mental Rehearsal** |

What effect would using the method(s) have on your whole performance?    4

**(20)**

## QUESTION 2

Choose **one** activity.

(a)    Describe your performance **strength(s)** in relation to **one** of the qualities from the list below.

| | | | |
|---|---|---|---|
| **Technical** | **Physical** | **Personal** | **Special** |

    4

(b)    Now select a different quality from the list below and describe your performance **weakness(es).**

| | | | |
|---|---|---|---|
| **Technical** | **Physical** | **Personal** | **Special** |

    4

(c)    Describe how you collected data about your performance.    4

(d)    Explain how you used this data to plan your improvement programme.    4

(e)    Why is it important to monitor your improvement programme?    4

**(20)**

## SECTION 2—PREPARATION OF THE BODY

*Marks*

**QUESTION 3**

Choose **one** activity.

(*a*)    Select **two** aspects of fitness.  Explain why each is important for a successful performance.                                                                                 5

(*b*)    Select **one** of the aspects of fitness from part (*a*).  Describe how you collected information on this aspect of fitness.                                                         3

(*c*)    Describe **one** method of training you have used to develop this aspect of fitness.                                                                                             4

(*d*)    Explain how your method of training helped to improve your whole performance.                                                                                               4

(*e*)    Explain why it is important to monitor your performance during training.            4

**(20)**

**QUESTION 4**

Choose **one** activity.

(*a*)    Describe a performance where Physical fitness **and** Skill Related fitness helped you perform successfully.                                                                     5

(*b*)    Describe **one** situation where Mental fitness affected your performance.            3

(*c*)    Select an aspect of fitness from **either** Physical, Skill Related **or** Mental fitness.  Describe a training programme you used to develop this aspect of fitness.                                                                                             4

(*d*)    Explain how you used the principles of training in your programme.                  4

(*e*)    Identify your future development needs.  Explain how these development needs may further improve your performance.                                                          4

**(20)**

**[Turn over**

## SECTION 3—SKILLS AND TECHNIQUES

*Marks*

### QUESTION 5

Choose **one** activity.

(a)   Describe **one** method you used to collect data about your **whole** performance.    4

(b)   Now describe **one** method you used to collect data about a **specific** skill in your performance.    3

(c)   Explain why both methods you used to collect data were appropriate.    4

(d)   Describe, in detail, an improvement programme you used to develop your skills and techniques.    5

(e)   Describe the changes to your whole performance, after completing your improvement programme.    4

**(20)**

### QUESTION 6

Choose **one** activity.

(a)   Describe the strengths and weaknesses in your performance.    4

(b)   Select a skill or technique you found difficult to perform.  Describe **two** methods of practice you used to develop this skill or technique.  Give specific examples.    4

(c)   What effect did the methods of practice have on your **whole** performance?    4

(d)   Explain how you used the principles of effective practice when developing your skill or technique.    4

(e)   Choose **one** of the factors from the list below.

**Motivation**          **Concentration**          **Feedback**

Explain why it was important in the development of the skill or technique in your performance.    4

**(20)**

### SECTION 4—STRUCTURES, STRATEGIES AND COMPOSITION

*Marks*

**QUESTION 7**

Choose **one** activity.

(*a*) Describe, in detail, your chosen structure, strategy or composition. **4**

(*b*) Describe how you gathered data on the effectiveness of your structure, strategy or composition. **4**

(*c*) Describe any problems you had when using the chosen structure, strategy or composition. **4**

(*d*) How would you change or adapt your structure, strategy or composition to develop your performance? **4**

(*e*) Explain the importance of decision making in relation to a structure, strategy or composition. Give examples. **4**

**(20)**

**QUESTION 8**

Choose **one** activity.

(*a*) Select a structure, strategy or composition. Describe the role you played or the performance you gave, within this structure, strategy or composition. **4**

(*b*) In your role, describe **one** weakness you had when performing the Structure, strategy or composition. **4**

(*c*) Explain the effect the weakness had on your whole performance. **4**

(*d*) What course of action did you take to improve your performance? **4**

(*e*) Following the course of action, how did you evaluate the effectiveness of your role or performance in the structure, strategy or composition? **4**

**(20)**

*[END OF QUESTION PAPER]*

[BLANK PAGE]

[BLANK PAGE]

# X205/201

| NATIONAL QUALIFICATIONS 2010 | TUESDAY, 1 JUNE 1.00 PM – 3.00 PM | PHYSICAL EDUCATION INTERMEDIATE 2 |

Candidates should attempt **THREE** questions, each chosen from a different section.

## SECTION 1—PERFORMANCE APPRECIATION

*Marks*

## QUESTION 1

Choose **one** activity.

(a)   Describe a model performance in that activity.    **4**

(b)   What are your **weaknesses** compared to the model performance described in part (a)?    **4**

(c)   Describe how your performance is affected by mental factors.    **4**

(d)   What have you done in training to make your performance like the model performance?  Give specific examples.    **5**

(e)   Explain how your performance improved as a result of your training programme.    **3**

**(20)**

## QUESTION 2

Choose **one** activity.

(a)   Describe the demands of a quality performance.    **4**

(b)   Describe, in detail, **one** method you used to gather data about your performance.    **4**

(c)   Describe how you used the data gathered to plan your training programme.    **4**

(d)   Why is it important to set short **and** long term goals when developing your performance?  Give examples.    **4**

(e)   Describe how you monitored your training programme.    **4**

**(20)**

## SECTION 2—PREPARATION OF THE BODY

*Marks*

## QUESTION 3

Choose **one** activity.

(a)    Describe, in detail, the fitness demands for your chosen activity.    **4**

(b)    Select **one** aspect of fitness from your chosen activity.  Describe how you assessed your level of fitness for this aspect.    **4**

(c)    How did the aspect of fitness, selected in part (b), affect your performance?    **4**

(d)    Describe, in detail, **one** method of training you used to develop this aspect of fitness.    **4**

(e)    Describe the effects that your training programme had on your performance.    **4**

**(20)**

## QUESTION 4

Choose **one** activity.

(a)    Choose **one** type of fitness from the list below.

  • **Physical fitness**
  • **Skill-related fitness**
  • **Mental fitness**

   Describe how this type of fitness can help you to perform successfully.    **4**

(b)    Choose a **different** type of fitness.  Explain how a weakness in this type of fitness affected your performance.    **4**

(c)    What principles of training did you consider when planning a training programme?    **4**

(d)    How did you apply these principles of training in your training programme?    **5**

(e)    Explain why it is important to monitor your training programme.    **3**

**(20)**

**[Turn over**

## SECTION 3—SKILLS AND TECHNIQUES

*Marks*

### QUESTION 5

Choose **one** activity.

(a)  Select a skill or technique.  Describe a model performance of your selected skill or technique.                                                                        **4**

(b)  Describe how you gathered information on your selected skill or technique.    **4**

(c)  Why were the method(s) used to gather information appropriate?               **3**

(d)  Describe, in detail, the programme of work you used to help your performance become more like the model performance.                                           **5**

(e)  Explain how a model performance can help you develop your whole performance.                                                                              **4**

**(20)**

### QUESTION 6

Choose **one** activity.

(a)  Describe the method(s) you used to gather information on your performance.     **4**

(b)  How did you use this information to plan an appropriate programme of work?     **4**

(c)  How did you ensure that the practices you used in your programme of work were effective?                                                                    **4**

(d)  Explain how you monitored the progress within your programme of work.        **4**

(e)  What would you now regard as your next development need?  What effect might this have on your performance?                                                 **4**

**(20)**

## SECTION 4—STRUCTURES, STRATEGIES AND COMPOSITION

*Marks*

### QUESTION 7

Choose **one** activity.

(*a*)   Select a structure, strategy or composition you have used.  Describe, in detail, your selected structure, strategy or composition.        **4**

(*b*)   Choose **one** element from the list below.

**Space        Speed        Variation        Motifs        Creativity**

**Design form        Width        Depth        Mobility**

Explain how this was a **strength** in your structure, strategy or composition.        **4**

(*c*)   Choose a **different** element from part (*b*).  Explain how this was a **weakness** in your structure, strategy or composition.        **4**

(*d*)   What decision(s) did you take to improve the effectiveness of your structure, strategy or composition?        **4**

(*e*)   Describe how the decision(s) you took made your whole performance more effective.        **4**

**(20)**

### QUESTION 8

Choose **one** activity.

(*a*)   Describe **your role/performance** within a structure, strategy or composition.        **4**

(*b*)   Describe, in detail, how you gathered information about **your role/performance** within the structure, strategy or composition.        **4**

(*c*)   From the information gathered describe any weakness(es) in your performance within the structure, strategy or composition.        **4**

(*d*)   What actions did you take to address the weakness(es) identified in part (*c*)?        **4**

(*e*)   How has your whole performance improved?        **4**

**(20)**

*[END OF QUESTION PAPER]*

[BLANK PAGE]

# 2011

[BLANK PAGE]

# X205/201

NATIONAL
QUALIFICATIONS
2011

MONDAY, 30 MAY
1.00 PM – 3.00 PM

PHYSICAL
EDUCATION
INTERMEDIATE 2

Candidates should attempt **THREE** questions, each chosen from a different section.

## SECTION 1—PERFORMANCE APPRECIATION

*Marks*

### QUESTION 1

Choose **one** activity.

(a) Choose **one** of the performance qualities from the list below.

- **Technical** (Timing, Consistency, Effectiveness and Refinement)
- **Physical** (Strong, Light)
- **Personal** (Motivation)
- **Special** (Flair, Imagination)

Describe your own performance with reference to your chosen quality.    **4**

(b) Choose a **different** performance quality from the list in part (a). Describe your own performance with reference to your chosen quality.    **4**

(c) Give examples of the goals you set yourself in order to reach a quality performance.    **4**

(d) Describe, in detail, a programme of work to develop/improve your performance qualities.    **5**

(e) Describe the quality of your performance after your programme of work.    **3**

**(20)**

### QUESTION 2

Choose **one** activity.

(a) Describe the range of performance qualities you would expect to have in your performance.    **4**

(b) Describe how you obtained information about your performance qualities.    **4**

(c) Using the information obtained in part (b), what are the strengths and weaknesses of your performance?    **4**

(d) How did you plan your training programme to improve the **weakness(es)** in your performance?    **4**

(e) Explain how you would evaluate your performance **after** you have completed your training programme.    **4**

**(20)**

## SECTION 2—PREPARATION OF THE BODY

*Marks*

**QUESTION 3**

Choose **one** activity.

(*a*) Describe the different types of fitness required for your chosen activity. 4

(*b*) Select **one** type of fitness from your chosen activity. Describe the method(s) you used to assess your level of fitness. 4

(*c*) Describe, in detail, the training you completed to improve your level of fitness. 5

(*d*) Explain why your training helped you to perform more effectively. Give examples to support your answer. 4

(*e*) How would you further develop your perfomance? 3

**(20)**

**QUESTION 4**

Choose **one** activity.

(*a*) Identify an aspect of fitness that you needed to improve. How did this aspect of fitness affect your performance? 4

(*b*) How did you use the principles of training when planning your programme? 5

(*c*) Describe a method of training you used to develop the aspect of fitness selected in part (*a*). 4

(*d*) How did you monitor your training programme? 4

(*e*) Explain the importance of monitoring your training programme. 3

**(20)**

**[Turn over**

## SECTION 3—SKILLS AND TECHNIQUES

*Marks*

## QUESTION 5

Choose **one** activity.

*(a)*   Describe, in detail, a skilled performance in this activity.    **5**

*(b)*   Select a skill or technique which was a weakness in your performance.  How did you gather information on this skill or technique?    **4**

*(c)*   How did the skill/technique selected in part *(b)* affect your whole performance?    **3**

*(d)*   Describe, in detail, a programme of work you used to improve the weakness selected in part *(b)*.    **5**

*(e)*   Describe how you monitored your progress during your programme of work.    **3**

**(20)**

## QUESTION 6

Choose **one** activity.

*(a)*   Describe, in detail, what you know about each of the stages of learning listed below.

**Preparation Stage (Cognitive)          Practice Stage (Associative)**

**Automatic Stage**    **5**

*(b)*   Describe **two** different methods of practice you used for **one** of the stages listed in *(a)*.    **4**

*(c)*   Select **two** of the factors listed below.

**Motivation          Concentration          Feedback**

Explain why they were important when carrying out your methods of practice.    **4**

*(d)*   Describe the improvements to your whole performance after progressing through the stages of learning.    **4**

*(e)*   What would you now consider to be your next steps in developing your performance?    **3**

**(20)**

## SECTION 4—STRUCTURES, STRATEGIES AND COMPOSITION

*Marks*

**QUESTION 7**

Choose **one** activity.

(a)    Select a structure, strategy or composition.

Describe how you gathered information on your performance in this structure, strategy or composition.                                    **4**

(b)    Explain why it is important to gather information on your structure, strategy or composition.                                          **3**

(c)    Select **two** of the elements below.

- **Speed**          • **Space**
- **Width**          • **Depth**
- **Mobility**       • **Variation**
- **Motif**          • **Creativity**

Explain why both are important in your structure, strategy or composition.   **5**

(d)    Describe in detail **one** situation where you experienced difficulties in your structure, strategy or composition.                        **4**

(e)    What did you do to overcome these difficulties?                          **4**

**(20)**

**[Turn over for Question 8 on *Page six***

## QUESTION 8

Choose **one** activity.

*Marks*

(*a*) Describe a structure, strategy or composition that you have used.    **4**

(*b*) Describe the strengths of your chosen structure, strategy or composition.    **4**

(*c*) Describe the weaknesses of your chosen structure, strategy or composition.    **4**

(*d*) Select **two** from the list below.

- **Being creative**
- **Making effective decisions under pressure**
- **Making good judgements**
- **Using information on team/individual performance**
- **Adapting/changing structure, strategy or composition**

Explain why both were important when applying the structure, strategy or composition described in part (*a*).    **5**

(*e*) Why is it important to evaluate your structure, strategy or composition?    **3**

**(20)**

*[END OF QUESTION PAPER]*

[BLANK PAGE]

# X205/11/02

| NATIONAL QUALIFICATIONS 2012 | TUESDAY, 29 MAY 1.00 PM – 3.00 PM | PHYSICAL EDUCATION INTERMEDIATE 2 |

Candidates should attempt **THREE** questions, each chosen from a different section.

## SECTION 1—PERFORMANCE APPRECIATION

*Marks*

### QUESTION 1

Choose **one** activity.

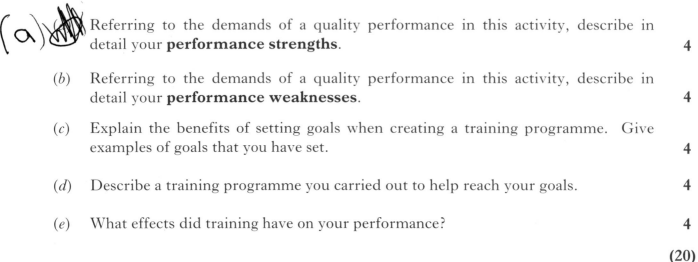

*(a)* Referring to the demands of a quality performance in this activity, describe in detail your **performance strengths**.    4

*(b)* Referring to the demands of a quality performance in this activity, describe in detail your **performance weaknesses**.    4

*(c)* Explain the benefits of setting goals when creating a training programme. Give examples of goals that you have set.    4

*(d)* Describe a training programme you carried out to help reach your goals.    4

*(e)* What effects did training have on your performance?    4

**(20)**

### QUESTION 2

Choose **one** activity.

*(a)* Describe the range of demands in a quality performance.    4

*(b)* Describe, in detail, **one** method you used to gather data on your performance.    4

*(c)* Mental factors can influence performance.

Give examples of situations where you were successful in managing your emotions.    4

*(d)* Give examples of different situations where you were unsuccessful in managing your emotions.    4

*(e)* Select **one** or **more** of the method(s) below:

- Imagery/visualisation
- Deep breathing
- Relaxation techniques
- Rehearsal

Describe how you used the method(s) to manage your emotions more effectively.    4

**(20)**

**SECTION 2—PREPARATION OF THE BODY**                    *Marks*

## QUESTION 3

Choose **one** activity.

(*a*)  Select **one** type of fitness from the list below.

- Physical fitness

- Skill related fitness

- Mental fitness

Explain why this type of fitness is a strength in your performance.                    **4**

(*b*)  Select a **different** type of fitness from the list in (*a*).  Explain why this type of fitness is a weakness in your performance.                    **4**

(*c*)  When developing your weakness, how did you use the principles of training during your training programme?                    **4**

(*d*)  Describe in detail how you monitored your training programme.                    **4**

(*e*)  Describe how your training programme changed over time.  Give examples to support your answer.                    **4**

                                                                        **(20)**

## QUESTION 4

Choose **one** activity.

(*a*)  (i)  Identify **one** aspect of fitness.  Explain why this was a **strength** in your performance.                    **3**

(ii)  Identify a **different** aspect of fitness.  Explain why this was a **weakness** in your performance.                    **3**

(*b*)  Describe a test you carried out to gather information on your weak aspect of fitness and explain why this test was useful.                    **4**

(*c*)  When you planned your training programme, describe the factors you considered to ensure its success.                    **4**

(*d*)  Identify a method of training you used in your training programme.  Describe a training session using this method.                    **3**

(*e*)  Explain the benefits of using this method of training.                    **3**

                                                                        **(20)**

## SECTION 3—SKILLS AND TECHNIQUES

*Marks*

### QUESTION 5

Choose **one** activity.

(a) Describe a method you used to collect data and explain why this method was appropriate.    **4**

(b) Select a skill or technique which was a strength. What effect did this have on your whole performance?    **4**

(c) Select a skill or technique which was a weakness. What effect did this have on your whole performance?    **4**

(d) Describe a programme of work you used to improve your weakness.    **4**

(e) Describe **two** different examples of feedback used during your programme of work.    **4**

**(20)**

### QUESTION 6

Choose **one** activity.

(a) Select a skill or technique that was a weakness.

Describe **two** different methods of practice you used to improve this skill or technique.    **4**

(b) How did you use the principles of effective practice in your programme of work?    **4**

(c) Select **one** of the factors below.

**Motivation**              **Concentration**              **Feedback**

Describe how you used the selected factor in your programme of work.    **4**

(d) Explain why you would evaluate your performance at the end of your programme of work.    **4**

(e) What effect did your programme of work have on your whole performance?    **4**

**(20)**

## SECTION 4—STRUCTURES, STRATEGIES AND COMPOSITION

*Marks*

### QUESTION 7

Choose **one** activity.

(a) Select a structure, strategy or composition. Describe your role/performance within the structure, strategy or composition.

**4**

(b) Explain why you were suited to this role/performance.

**4**

(c) Describe some of the problems experienced when using the structure, strategy or composition.

**4**

(d) Describe the course of action you took to minimise the problems described in part (c).

**4**

(e) Give examples of what you would work on next. Describe how this would further develop your performance.

**4**

**(20)**

### QUESTION 8

Choose **one** activity.

(a) Describe a structure, strategy or composition.

**4**

(b) Explain the benefits of the structure, strategy or composition.

**4**

(c) Describe the limitations you experienced when using your chosen structure, strategy or composition.

**4**

(d) How did you adapt or change your structure, strategy or composition to improve the effectiveness of your performance?

**4**

(e) Describe how this affected your performance.

**4**

**(20)**

*[END OF QUESTION PAPER]*

[BLANK PAGE]

# INTERMEDIATE 2 | ANSWER SECTION

To help you most when using this answer section, look at each part of the question, then look at the paragraph after 'A good response …'. Use this material to help to plan your answer. Check if you have put in the suggestions made and then justified them. The example answers are very helpful but you must be able to change them to suit the activity you are going to use.

## INTERMEDIATE 2 PHYSICAL EDUCATION 2008

In relation to **all** questions it should be noted that the relevance of the content in the candidates' responses will depend on:

- the activity selected
- the performance focus
- the training/development programme/programme of work selected
- the practical experiences of their course as the contexts for answers.

### PERFORMANCE APPRECIATION

**1.** (a) *A good response should include some or most of the points as outlined below. To demonstrate acquired knowledge and understanding the candidate's response should include an outline of the range of qualities expected in a model performer.*

#### Qualities
In relation to any of the qualities selected a description should be offered of a quality performance. Candidates may demonstrate acquired knowledge and understanding in respect of:

**Technical qualities**: Think about a repertoire of skills, for example *dribbling, passing, shooting, and so on is consistent and accurate*. This may be accompanied by clarification of success rate or quality of execution or PAR. Reference may also be made to the classification of skills demanded, e.g. simple/complex etc.

**Physical qualities**: Think about more than one aspect of fitness. To support acquired or applied knowledge and understanding the candidate must describe how the selected aspect of fitness affects quality performance. For example, *high levels of cardio respiratory endurance, speed endurance helped maintain pace and track my opponents continuously …*

**Personal qualities**: Think about inherent qualities, for example *qualities such as being determined or confident or competitive (and so on), helped because opponents felt threatened …*

**Special qualities**: Think about the ability to create opportunity, deceive opponents, make performance look more dynamic, apply flair, have the ability to choreograph routines, link skills and so on.
For example, *these unique qualities helped to fake intent and so wrong-foot opponents …the routine was exciting to watch …this helped gain more points* etc.

(b) *A good response should include some or most of the points as outlined below.*

#### The use of model performance
A good response will include reference to the appropriateness of model performance, when developing their personal improvement plan. Most likely this will relate to skill learning or development. For example, using a model performer can advantage performance in a number of ways:

- Identify strengths and weaknesses.
- Increase confidence and/or motivation.
- Provide various types of feedback.
- Provide challenge in practice or competition.
- Provide accurate feeds continuously.
- Inspire to achieve higher levels of achievement.
- Support planning practice/targets.
- Inspire to copy ideas.

For example, *I watched a model performer in my class … It made me want to be as good as they were. When practising my right hand lay-up I got feedback from them and they were my opponent in a 1 v 1 challenge … this helped as a form of target setting; this kept me motivated and determined to do better … I gained in confidence and felt that my technique had greatly improved as a result.*

(c) *A good response should include some or most of the points as outlined below. The candidate should demonstrate a level of critical thinking when describing their weakness.*

#### Strengths and weaknesses
The responses will be relevant to the activity selected. Candidates may demonstrate acquired knowledge and understanding in respect of the specific role or team/solo responsibilities, strengths and weaknesses. Most likely, a relevant analysis in relation to the identified technical, physical, personal and special strengths and weaknesses may be evident in the candidates' answer.

Merit should be given according to quality of description(s) and explanation(s) offered.

(d) *A good response should include some or most of the points as outlined below. The candidate's response should include detailed discussion to demonstrate thorough knowledge and understanding about the importance of goal setting.*

#### Setting goals
A response will give examples of specific short- and long-term goals set. For example, *I decided to set myself a short-term goal of increasing my power. My long-term goal would be to use this effectively when spiking in volleyball.*

(e) *A good response should include some or most of the points as outlined below. The candidate should be able to show acquired knowledge.*

#### Monitoring training using particular methods
Methods used could include: video, observation schedules, training diary, logbook, personal evaluation or game/performance analysis.

**2.** (a) *A good response should include some or most of the points as outlined below. The candidate's response should include full details with relevant examples to demonstrate acquired knowledge and understanding. It is perfectly acceptable for the candidate to offer from an individual/team perspective.*

#### Demands
Technical, physical, mental and special. Candidates may demonstrate acquired knowledge and understanding across all related demands or focus on one with more detail. Similarly, candidates may demonstrate acquired knowledge and understanding in respect of the unique game/event or emphasise the challenges unique to the role. They may refer

to: the duration of the game and/or event; codes of conduct; whether the venue (indoor/outdoor) affects performance; directly/indirectly competitive; the scoring systems (objective/subjective) and so on.

The responses will be wide ranging and relevant to the activity selected. Candidates may demonstrate acquired knowledge and understanding in respect of the specific role- or solo-related demands necessary for an effective performance.

Reference to the application of a series of challenges/skills will impact on performance in competitive situations. For example:

- In relation to **role** – *as a central midfielder I have to keep going for the whole game. If I get tired and time my tackle wrong we could lose the game because I might give away a penalty because of fouls. I have to be accurate and agile so that I can dummy my opponent so that I can pass straight to my team or make space for myself ... and so on.*
- In relation to **solo challenges** – *as a gymnast I know that my tumbling routine has many skills that need to be performed in a linked sequence ... I need to focus as I will be pushing myself to the limits ... most importantly I need to add flair and fluency in my routine to gain more marks from the judges ... and so on.*

(b) *A good response should include some or most of the points as outlined below. To demonstrate acquired knowledge and understanding the candidate's response should select **two** of the qualities and explain how they affected performance.*

**Qualities**
In relation to any of the qualities selected, a description should be offered of a quality performance. Candidates may demonstrate acquired knowledge and understanding in respect of:

**Technical qualities**: Think about a repertoire of skills, for example *dribbling, passing, shooting (and so on) is consistent and accurate.* This may be accompanied by clarification of success rate or quality of execution or PAR. Reference may also be made to the classification of skills demanded, e.g. simple/complex etc.

**Physical qualities**: Think about more than one aspect of fitness. To support acquired or applied knowledge and understanding, the candidate must describe how the selected aspect of fitness affects quality performance. For example, *high levels of cardio respiratory endurance, speed endurance helped maintain pace and track my opponents continuously ...*

**Personal qualities**: Think about inherent qualities, for example *qualities such as being determined or confident or competitive ... helped because opponents felt threatened ...*

**Special qualities**: Think about the ability to create opportunity, deceive opponents, make performance look more dynamic, apply flair, have the ability to choreograph routines, link skills, and so on.
For example, *these unique qualities helped to fake intent and so wrong-foot opponents ... The routine was exciting to watch ... This helped gain more points etc.*

(c) *A good response should include some or most of the points as outlined below. The candidate's response should include full detail with relevant examples to demonstrate applied knowledge and understanding from the training used.*

**Course of action**
A good response will include details relevant to the selection and appropriateness of the **most** relevant methods of practice or development or training available. Examples relevant to selected methods and how this will bring about

improvement, making the performance more like a model performer, must be evident.

For example, *to make sure my lay-up shot was more like a model performer, I used many repetition drills with no pressure ... I then progressed to a practice, which needed more decisions and used combination/conditioned drills to make the shot more effective ... Against opposition I was more confident, accurate ... and so on.*

(d) *A good response should include some or most of the points as outlined below. The candidate's response should include specific examples of how mental factors affected training.*

**Mental factors – related improvement techniques**
Candidates may demonstrate acquired knowledge and understanding by referencing some of the following: the ability to manage emotions; dealing with anxiety; level of arousal (over or under); handling stress; effect of self confidence; motivation; concentration, and so on.

The candidate may suggest the influences on training being positive/negative. The candidate should highlight the specific aspect of mental fitness, such as: dealing with anxiety, managing emotions; level of arousal (over or under) etc. The selected factor must be relevant and the effect on training justified. For example, *I found it difficult to concentrate on a practice because it didn't seem as important as when I was in the game ... and so on.*

(e) *A good response should include some or most of the points as outlined below.*

**Course effectiveness/impact on performance development**
A good response **must** include evaluative comments and offer examples on how and why the candidate thought the course of action taken was effective. For example, *as I practised in both closed and open contexts this helped me to practise with and without pressure ... This helped me to gain confidence and so on.* The candidate could state what the impact of skill/technique development to **whole** performance development was. For example, *I became a more consistent shooter with higher shooting average ... or more points won, a positive benefit including greater confidence ... better help to team etc.*

## PREPARATION OF THE BODY

3. (a) *A good response should include some or most of the points as outlined below. The candidate must demonstrate acquired knowledge and understanding in the description of how **each** type of fitness contributes to effective performance within the selected activity.*

**Physical fitness**: For example, *in badminton CRE is needed to last long rallies and keep my skill level high the whole time. Speed and strength are important to give power so that the smash is difficult to return.*
**Skill-related fitness**: For example, *in badminton having good agility will allow me quick movement ... to reach the shuttle or change direction if necessary and return the shuttle to put my opponent under pressure ... good timing will allow me to hit the shuttle at the correct time, giving me more chance to win a point because my opponent struggles to return it.*
**Mental fitness**: For example, *in badminton I need to be able to concentrate for the whole match ... concentrate on each shot ... being focussed ... be determined to win ... not being distracted etc.*

(b) *A good response should include some or most of the points as outlined below. The candidate must select an appropriate aspect and give a description as to how they gathered assessed that aspect of fitness.*

## Accurate collection and recording of data

**Gathering data**: The description of the method could be within or outwith the activity. A diagram may feature in the answer, for example a time-related observation schedule within football that shows information relevant to the particular aspect selected (speed and cardio respiratory endurance). In the answer the candidate may make reference to the process as to how the information was gathered. A narrative account of what was done and **why** should be obvious, showing logical thinking. Methods could include: video performance profiles, stroke/breath/pulse counts and feedback.

Methods could come from outwith the activity or standardised tests may also be described, these could include:

- Physical – 12 minute Cooper test, sit and reach test, Harvard step test, bleep test.
- Skill related – Illinois agility test, ruler drop, alternate hand throw.
- Mental – Questionnaires or self evaluation tests, internal/external feedback.

(c) *A good response should include some or most of the points as outlined below. The candidate must demonstrate both acquired and applied knowledge to why specific fitness needs require to be identified before planning a training programme.*

**Specificity to activity**: For example, *in dance I require to have good flexibility and therefore I would base my programme around stretching exercises.*

**Person**: For example, *I only achieved a below average score for my agility, therefore I must base the start of my training programme at a suitable level.*

**Performance**: For example, *in order to improve my agility during my game performance, I had to make sure I incorporated some game-like agility drills into my programme.*

(d) *A good response should include some or most of the points as outlined below. The candidate must describe and give examples of specific fitness needs.*

### Role-related fitness

A response should include reference to the activity selected, and be able to show both acquired and applied knowledge of the role-related fitness requirements. Suggestions may be made about the types of fitness, i.e. physical, skill related and mental.

**Physical fitness**: For example, *in hockey I play as a midfielder ... my cardio respiratory endurance is poor ... as I am unable to support both attacking and defensive play ... when my team is attacking I need to be just behind strikers ... I fail to give this support ... I am therefore going to work on increasing my CRE*

**Skill-related fitness**: For example, *in hockey I do not have good timing and balance ... I am unable to time the pass when I have the ball ... so it is hit without the correct speed and accuracy ... to reach my team ... I am going to set a specific training programme to work on my timing and speed.*

(e) *A good response should include some or most of the points as outlined below. The candidate must describe the course of action taken.*

A good response should have a description of the form of training for the selected approach.

**In the activity (conditioning)**: Fartlek short sprints and then continuous paced running with a description of what they did. For example, *in athletics, for 800 metre running, I did Fartlek training ... did eight laps, jogged the straights and ran the bends ... this was done without stopping ... then did six*

short 60 metre sprints ... a short 20 metre jog leading into each sprint made the demand similar to end of an actual race.

**Outwith the activity**: Could include circuit training or weight training with description of what they did sets/reps or types of exercise. For example, *to improve my cardio respiratory endurance for my role as a midfielder in hockey ... I trained outwith the activity ... carried out some circuit training.*

**Combination of both**: Continuous training in pool and weight training out of pool with an appropriate description of each, involving some of the following methods: Fartlek, continuous, conditioning, interval, circuit, weight training, relaxation, breathing or rehearsal.

For example, *in swimming I trained using a combination of training within activity and outwith the activity ... within I used interval training ... did warm up ... then stroke improvement ... main set 6 × 50 metre swim with 1 minute recovery ... subset 6 × 50 with 45 secs recovery ... then warm down. Outwith the pool I did a weight training circuit ... doing a series of exercises ... three sets of exercises ... also some work on stepping machines ... rowing machines ... to improve cardio respiratory endurance and so on.*

The candidate may also refer to the length of the training programme, progressive overload, frequency, intensity, duration, adaptation, rest/recovery, targets they set themselves.

**4.** (a) *A good response should include some or most of the points as outlined below. The candidate must describe in detail a training programme used to develop an aspect of fitness.*

**In the activity (conditioning)**: Fartlek short sprints and then continuous paced running with a description of what they did. For example, *in athletics, for 800 metre running, I did Fartlek training ... did eight laps, jogged the straights and ran the bends ... this was done without stopping ... then did six short 60 metre sprints ... a short 20 metre jog leading into each sprint made the demand similar to end of an actual race.*

**Outwith the activity**: Could include circuit training or weight training with description of what they did sets/reps or types of exercise. For example, *to improve my cardio respiratory endurance for my role as a midfielder in hockey ... I trained outwith the activity ... carried out some circuit training.*

**Combination of both**: Continuous training in pool and weight training out of pool with an appropriate description of each, involving some of the following methods: Fartlek, continuous, conditioning, interval, circuit, weight training, relaxation, breathing or rehearsal.

For example, *in swimming I trained using a combination of training within activity and outwith the activity ... within I used interval training ... did warm up ... then stroke improvement ... main set 6 × 50 metre swim with 1 minute recovery ... subset 6 × 50 with 45 seconds of recovery ... then warm down. Outwith the pool I did a weight training circuit ... doing a series of exercises ... three sets of exercises ... also some work on stepping machines ... rowing machines ... to improve cardio respiratory endurance and so on.*

The candidate may also refer to the length of the training programme, progressive overload, frequency, intensity, duration, adaptation, rest/recovery, targets they set themselves.

(b) *A good response should include some or most of the points as outlined below. The candidate must demonstrate acquired knowledge in how they applied the principles of training to their programme.*

### Principles of training

The answer must refer to the principles of training. Most of the following principles should be referred to: specificity to activity, person and performance, progressive overload, frequency, intensity, duration, adaptation, rest/recovery, over training, reversibility. You will probably have a description of how they were applied to the programme and also an explanation and justification of why they were considered.

For example, *I made sure the training was specific to the weakness identified … also demands of activity … I trained three times per week with rest every other … allowed body to recover … applied overload after week 3 … increased number of sets … training became harder and body adapted to new load … as I was getting fitter … variety within programme … prevent boredom and keep motivation high.*

(c) *A good response should include some or most of the points as outlined below. The candidate must demonstrate both acquired and applied knowledge and understanding when monitoring the effectiveness of their training programme.*

### Monitoring training

Methods used could include: video, observation schedules, training diary, logbook, personal evaluation or game/performance analysis.

For example, *I used a training diary … this allowed me to keep a note of my progress … allowed me to see whether my training was working … if I had achieved my short term goals … if my training had been set at the correct level … to know when to increase my workload … to see if my overall performance had improved.*

(d) *A good response should include some or most of the points as outlined below. The candidate must demonstrate relevant knowledge and understanding and show critical thinking about the importance of monitoring their training programme.*

### The monitoring process

A response will show knowledge about the purpose and importance of the process. It may provide qualitative or quantitative details of whether the training is effective/working. It can support the specific fitness progress. Explanations may include: providing evidence to compare progress; targets; improvements; enabling changes to be made; ensuring future targets; further challenges and promoting motivation. Could also offer whether training method was appropriate; deciding if training was at correct intensity and whether short- or long-term goals had been achieved.

(e) *A good response should include some or most of the points as outlined below. The candidate must demonstrate relevant knowledge and understanding and show critical thinking regarding the effect training had on their performance.*

### Impact on performance

For example, *during my basketball game my improved level of CRE … allowed me to keep up with my player, even in later stages of the game … I was still able to get back quickly to defend … was able to maintain a high level of performance throughout the game.* The evidence must relate to the whole performance, with relevant answers given.

## SKILLS AND TECHNIQUES

5. (a) *A good response should include some or most of the points as outlined below. The candidate's response should demonstrate acquired knowledge and understanding in describing a skilled performance.*

### Features of a skilled performance

A link to relevant factors may include: a repertoire of skills evident and executed at the correct time with consistency, fluency etc.; movements or application of skills seeming effortless; management of emotions is controlled; degree of confidence; few unforced errors; making appropriate decisions when under pressure.

Ability to vary and adapt by using a range of skills and techniques, considering the correct options for the various performance demands.

(b) *A good response should include some or most of the points as outlined below. The candidate should make comparisons from their own performance to that of the skilled performance*

### Features of a skilled performance

A good response may suggest the range and qualities that are evident in their performance as compared to a skilled/model performance, – technical, physical, and/or mental related. A link to other relevant factors may include a repertoire of skills evident, for example, *unlike the skilled performance I am unable to carry out a range of skills, I am unable to carry out a backhand clear or a drop shot … I do not always carry out my skills with consistency, fluency etc., unlike that of a skilled performance … in a skilled performance, movements or application of skills seem effortless, whereas I use up a lot of energy to carry out the basic skills … I am unable to vary and adapt by using a range of skills and techniques or consider the correct options for the various performance demands.*

The candidate may opt to use his response from part (a) to assist with this question.

(c) *A good response should include some or most of the points as outlined below. The candidate's response should demonstrate a description of how they planned a programme of improvement.*

### Practice considerations

A good response may include details relevant to the selection and appropriateness of the most relevant methods of practice, development or training available. Considerations of different methods will be evident in the process. Examples relevant to selected methods will be included, highlighting the selections made.

- At the cognitive stage – *many shadow or repetition practices were incorporated.*
- At the associative stage – *some shadow or repetition practices, progressing to combination drills.*
- At the automatic stage of learning – *more pressure or problem-solving drills were used to advance and challenge learning and performance development.*

A link to other relevant factors may include: whole part gradual build up, closed/open contexts etc.

### Programme of work

The responses offered will depend on the candidate's choice of skill/technique identified for development.

The response may include details of the appropriateness of the methods of practice or development programme followed. The programme followed should refer to some of the following considerations: stages of learning, skill complexity, skill classification, model performer, feedback, goal setting and so on.

Programme references may include details of weeks 1 and 2, weeks 3 and 4, weeks 5 and 6, etc. Or, *I used a gradual build up /whole part whole approach to my development programme.* In this respect the notion of reliability and validity should be apparent and justified etc.

The content and structure given must be justified with progressions exemplified to demonstrate sound knowledge and understanding. For example, *as I was at the cognitive stage, I used many shadow and repetition practices to ensure … At the associative stage I used some shadow and repetition practices … At the automatic stage of learning I knew to use more pressure as this would challenge me more … I found the [chosen] skill very difficult so decided to use gradual build up as this would … In weeks 1 and 2 I concentrated more on simple drills … in weeks 3 and 4, I progressed to more complex drills such as … this built my confidence as I reached my target of … and so on.*

A link to other relevant factors may include: whole part, gradual build up, closed/open contexts, repetitions, target setting, model performers etc.

(d) *A good response should include some or most of the points as outlined below. The candidate's response should discuss how the improvement programme helped the **whole** performance.*

### Whole performance development
The responses offered may suggest the impact of improved skill/technique development to whole performance effectiveness. For example, a more consistent application, fewer errors, more points won, a positive benefit including greater confidence etc.

The candidate may also include details referencing specific drills or parts of the programme that benefited their performance, for example *I felt that the repetition drills such as … improved my ability to … and so on.*

Merit will be given to the feasibility, validity and/or justification for claims of improved performance.

(e) *A good response should include some or most of the points as outlined below.*

The candidate should identify a future development need to further improve their performance. A good response will show how they identified this future development need, what specific difficulties they had and a summary of how they intended to work on this.

6. (a) *A good response should include some or most of the points as outlined below.*
A good response will include reference to specific parts that the candidate had difficulty in performing. Link to other relevant factors such as: breaking the skill down into preparation, action, recovery; execution with the correct time; with consistency, fluency; eases of economy; movements/application of skill seem effortless.

(b) *A good response should include some or most of the points as outlined below. The candidate's response should describe the methods used to analyse the weakness identified in part (a).*

### Gathering information on performance strengths or weaknesses
The responses will be wide ranging and relevant to the activity selected but points raised should be justified.

A link to identified strengths and/or weaknesses may be evident. A good response will include reference to whole performance (initial data) and specific (focused data). To support claims, reference should be made to one or more of the following:
- Movement analysis – observation checklist, match analysis sheet, preparation/action/recovery.
- Mechanical analysis – study of force, balance, centre of gravity etc.

- Consideration of quality – reflection on whether your skill or technique was controlled, fluent, or fast/slow.
- Video – comparison of your performance with that of a model performer.

(c) *A good response should include some or most of the points as outlined below. The candidate's response should demonstrate knowledge and understanding in their description of the methods of practice used to develop the identified skill or technique.*

Methods of practice: Give detailed examples of the methods of practice you have used to develop the skill/technique. For example, shadow practice and combination drill; *for shadow practice I went through the action of the smash without a shuttle. I did this five times and got feedback from my partner.*

(d) *A good response should include some or most of the points as outlined below. The candidate must use critical thinking to explain why the methods were useful in improving their weakness.*

- At the cognitive stage – *I used shadow or repetition practices, as I was able to practice my skill without pressure of actually hitting the ball … I was able to focus on the sub-routines.*
- At the associative stage – *I progressed to combination drills, which allowed me to practice in a more game-like situation.*
- At the automatic stage of learning – *more pressure or problem-solving drills were used to advance and challenge learning and performance development.*

A link to other relevant factors may include whole part gradual build up: *this helped me to build up a difficult, challenging skill in stages, allowing me to gain more confidence.*

(e) *A good response should include some or most of the points as outlined below. The candidate must select either motivation, concentration or feedback and explain its importance in their performance.*

### Motivation/concentration/feedback
In this respect the candidate may give a synopsis of how one of the factors selected impacted upon their learning and/or their application of skill/technique in the overall performance. Merit should be given according to relevance of explanations offered.

**Motivation**: A good response may include details of being internally/externally motivated to learn or achieve success. Being motivated enables the performer to· be self driven; listen to instruction and act on it; be self determined; give of their best; come from behind; respond to immediate problems or competitive challenges; not worry if mistakes are made and re channel focus.

**Concentration**: A good response may include details of the need to concentrate/focus on instruction or demonstration offered in order to: ensure effective application of skill or technique; promote progression or adaptation of skill or technique; ensure bad habits are not formed; enable the performer to perform their role and apply their skills appropriately.
In the context of games, concentration enables the performer to stick to role-related duties, and so on.

**Feedback**: A good response will include details of receiving internal feedback to progress or refine skill/technique; receiving/giving external feedback (visual/verbal/written to progress/refine skill/ technique of self or that of others). Feedback should be positive and immediate to promote confidence and/or success.

## STRUCTURES, STRATEGIES AND COMPOSITIONS

7.  (a) *A good response should include some or most of the points as outlined below. The candidate must demonstrate acquired knowledge and understanding regarding the structure, strategy or composition selected and be able explain why it was important to gather information.*

    ### The ability to pre-plan strategies to meet demands
    The responses will depend on the choice of structure, strategy or composition selected. Responses will include some of the following: strengths and weaknesses of own team; strengths and weaknesses of the opposition; particular strengths of individual players within the structure; strategy or composition; experience of players in team or opposition; previous results; how long one can apply the structure; strategy or composition; score in the game; time in the game; weather or ground conditions; amount of space to perform in; type of music or apparatus selected.

    (b) *A good response should include some or most of the points as outlined below.*

    Methods to gather information the effectiveness of the SSC may include video analysis, observation schedules, knowledge of results, personal reflection, internal/external feedback.

    (c) *A good response should include some or most of the points as outlined below. The candidate must be able to explain why their strengths and weaknesses affected the SSC.*

    ### The benefits of various systems of play
    For example:
    *In football a 3–5–2 formation is easier to dominate midfield … can cover wide areas of pitch … has a variety of attack options linking midfield and forwards.*
    *In volleyball … the specialist setter in our team was excellent … he/she was agile to receive passes … seldom gave up … consistently played an accurate ball … always communicated with others in the team.*

    ### Limitations of various SSC
    The responses will be wide ranging and will depend on the choice of SSC selected. Responses should start with a description of the problems faced, for example … *in basketball my 2–1–2 zone defence can be exposed by my opponents having a strong outside shooter, who could consistently score from outside the key … in my 4–4–2 my opponents played a long ball over the top of our defence, allowing an opportunity … and so on.*

    (d) *A good response should include some or most of the points as outlined below. The candidate must demonstrate relevant critical thinking and decision making to explain the actions they took to improve the effectiveness of their performance.*

    ### The importance of adapting and refining a structure, strategy or composition in response to performance demands
    The responses will depend on the choice of structure, strategy or composition selected. Responses could start with a brief description of the problem faced, then show evidence of problem solving and decision making to make their performance more effective. The candidate may decide to change structure, strategy or composition completely. For example, *in basketball we were playing a 2–1–2 zone … opposition had good outside shooters … scored frequently … we changed to half court man-to-man defence to stop them … we picked up our players at the half court … always made sure we were basket side … marked tightly when they attempted to shoot this led to fewer successful shots as they were under more pressure …. forced them to try and drive to*

basket. *They made more mistakes … scored fewer baskets as they were poor at driving to basket … we won more turnovers and could attack more.*

### Programme of work
They will describe a programme of work, taking cognisance of weaknesses described previously: a range of programmes may be offered including practising parts in isolation and/or unopposed/opposed practices/games. The content and structure must be justified with possible progressions within programme to explain the actions.
Candidates may also change or adapt the SSC either as individuals or as a team as a short term measure.

(e) *A good response should include some or most of the points as outlined below. The candidate should show acquired knowledge and understanding and relate to the effect their actions had on individual changes and whole performance.*

Candidate may choose to discuss the positive effects the actions had on their performance. For example, *we were now able to mark much tighter, which led to fewer baskets being scored; or as we changed our centre pass strategy we were able to pass the ball more effectively and quickly to our shooter, who had more opportunities to score.*

8.  (a) *A good response should include some or most of the points as outlined below. The candidate must demonstrate applied knowledge and understanding when describing a SSC in detail.*

    ### Select a relevant structure, strategy or composition
    The candidate must describe the structure, strategy or composition. Some will also make reference to the role they played.
    These could include:
    - Basketball – fast break, zones, 1–3–1, horseshoe offence, man-to-man defence.
    - Football – 4–2–4 or 4–3–3 or 3–5–2.
    - Badminton – front and back or sides.
    - Gymnastics – particular sequence/routine.
    - Volleyball – rotation.
    - Hockey – penalty corner.
    - Dance – a particular dance or routine used.

    For example, *in tennis I used a serve–volley strategy. I would serve fast and hard to opponent, follow my serve, get into net and quickly use a volley to win the point from the opponent's return.*

    (b) *A good response should include some or most of the points as outlined below. The candidate must demonstrate applied knowledge and understanding when describing the programme of work they went through to learn the SSC.*

    ### Programme of work
    They will describe a programme of work taking into account how the SSC was learned: a range of programmes may be offered, including practising parts in isolation and/or unopposed/ opposed practices/games. The content and structure must be justified, with possible progressions within the programme to explain the actions.

    (c) *A good response should include some or most of the points as outlined below. The candidate should select **one** factor and explain the importance of this factor in their SSC.*

    ### Structure and strategy fundamentals
    The following may be referred to or listed: using space in attack and defence; tempo of play; speed in attack; delay in defence and principles of play (width; depth and mobility). The importance should be justified and show both acquired and applied knowledge.

    For example, *in basketball it is important to play a fast tempo game … attack quickly … so I made sure that on each opportunity we tried to play a fast break ... to catch the defence out ... score a quick basket ... create an overload situation ... before the defence was organised properly.*

*In dance it is important to start with a simple step motif.*

### Structure and compositional fundamentals

The following may be referred to or listed: design form – developing motifs; linking movements; using space effectively. The importance should be justified and show both acquired and applied knowledge.

For example, *in dance I started with a simple step motif ... took me forwards then back to starting position ... then sideways ... back to starting ... I established this as a simple core motif ... then I developed a second core motif ... this time a jumping pattern ... then I began to mix and play with both core motifs ... to add interest to my dance ... gave my dance variety and quality of movement contrasts.*

(d) *A good response should include some or most of the points as outlined below. The candidate must explain why it is important to continually monitor their SSC.*

### Monitoring

It provides evidence to compare progress/targets/ improvements; aids motivation; gives evidence on whether programme of work carried out has been effective; checks whether training methods were appropriate; ensures progress and further development; gives feedback on your performance; ensures training at correct intensity; checks if improvements were made in areas/weaknesses you targeted; makes sure you are not overworking; analyses your training on an ongoing basis; provides information to plan adjustments to your training.

(e) *A good response should include some or most of the points as outlined below.*

The candidate should identify a future development need from to further improve their SSC. A good response will show how they identified this future development need, what specific difficulties they had and a summary of how they intended to work on this.

# INTERMEDIATE 2 PHYSICAL EDUCATION 2009

In relation to **all** questions it should be noted that the relevance of the content in the candidates' responses will depend on:

- the activity selected
- the performance focus
- the training/development programme/programme of work selected
- the practical experiences of their course as the contexts for answers.

## PERFORMANCE APPRECIATION

1. (a) *A good response should include some or most of the points as outlined below. To demonstrate acquired knowledge and understanding, the candidate's response should include a detailed description of a quality performance.*

### Qualities

In relation to any of the qualities selected, a description should be offered of a quality performance. Candidates may demonstrate acquired knowledge and understanding in respect of:

**Technical qualities**: Think about a repertoire of skills, e.g. that *dribbling, passing, shooting etc. is consistent and accurate.* This may be accompanied by a clarification of success rate **or** quality of execution **or** PAR. Reference may also be made to the classification of skills demanded, e.g. simple/complex etc.

**Physical qualities**: Think about more than one aspect of fitness. To support acquired or applied knowledge and understanding, the candidate must describe how the selected aspect of fitness affects quality performance. For example: *High levels of **cardio respiratory endurance, speed endurance** helped me maintain pace and track my opponents continuously ... and so on.*

**Personal qualities**: Think about inherent qualities. For example: *being determined/ confident/competitive helped because opponents felt threatened, and so on.*

**Special qualities**: Think about the ability to create opportunity, deceive opponents, make performances look more dynamic, apply flair, have the ability to choreograph routines, link skills ... etc. For example, *these unique qualities helped to fake intent and so wrong-foot opponents; the routine was exciting to watch ... this helped gain more points* etc.

(b) *A good response should include some or most of the points as outlined below. To demonstrate acquired knowledge and understanding the candidates should outline a goal they have set themselves.*

### Setting goals

A response will give examples of specific short- and long-term goals that were set. For example, *I decided to set myself a short-term goal of increasing my power. My long-term goal would be to use this effectively when spiking in volleyball.*

(c) *A good response should include some or most of the points as outlined below. The candidate should demonstrate acquired and applied knowledge and understanding in describing the improvement programme they have used to achieve their goal.*

### Course of action

A good response will include details relevant to the selection and appropriateness of the **most** relevant methods of practice or development or training available. Examples

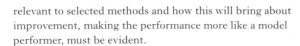

relevant to selected methods and how this will bring about improvement, making the performance more like a model performer, must be evident.

For example, *to make sure my lay-up shot was more like a model performer, I used many repetition drills with no pressure … I then progressed to a practice, which needed more decisions and used combination/ conditioned drills to make the shot more effective … Against opposition I was more confident, accurate … and so on.*

(d) *A good response should include some or most of the points as outlined below. Candidates may demonstrate acquired knowledge and understanding by choosing two factors and explaining why these factors affected their performance. The candidate may offer suggestions about the influences on performance being positive/negative.*

### Positive and negative influences of mental factors

A good response will suggest the potential effects that positive and negative mental factors will have on performance.

**Positive and negative influences of mental factors**: A good response will suggest the potential effects that positive and negative mental factors will have on performance.

For example, a **positive influence** will impact upon performance by improving state of mind – increasing state of arousal and so enabling the performer to handle the pressure and remain calm or make appropriate decisions and enable appropriate actions in response to the immediate situation. There may be improved awareness, confidence, fewer unforced errors, sustained performance standards and application of skills to deal with the performance context.

A **negative influence** will impact performance in producing an ineffective, erratic, unconfident performance. Other points raised may include apprehension/the feeling of defeat before the event has begun etc.

A link to other relevant factors may include: bad temper; nervousness, lack of commitment, committing fouls, over confidence, lack of confidence, etc.

(e) *A good response should include some or most of the points as outlined below.*

*Candidates may demonstrate acquired knowledge and understanding by choosing two factors and explaining the effect of **one** or **more** of the methods had on their whole performance.*

The candidate should highlight the specific method, such as: dealing with anxiety, managing emotions, level of arousal (over or under arousal) etc. Accompanying the examples offered, there should be good explanation to exhibit applied knowledge and understanding in context. For example, *as part of my warm up I used deep breathing, self talk, mental rehearsal and visualisation to keep me calm.*
Crucially the candidate must justify why the selected method(s) were appropriate: *self talk was appropriate as it is quick to use – key/trigger words give me a boost; concentration is increased … visualisation helps me go over in my mind how to complete the shot … I can do this quickly, focus my concentration and 'see in my head' the shot going in … and so on.*

2. (a) *A good response should include some or most of the points as outlined below. The candidate should demonstrate a level of critical thinking when describing their strengths in relation to **one** of the qualities.*

### Strengths

The responses will be relevant to the activity selected. Candidates may demonstrate acquired knowledge and understanding in respect of the specific role or team/solo responsibilities and strengths. A relevant analysis in relation to the identified technical, physical, personal and special strengths should be evident in the candidate's answer.

(b) *A good response should include some or most of the points as outlined below. The candidate should demonstrate a level of critical thinking when describing their strengths in relation to one of the qualities.*

### Weaknesses

The responses will be relevant to the activity selected. Candidates may demonstrate acquired knowledge and understanding in respect of the specific role or team/solo responsibilities, weakness(es). A relevant analysis in relation to the identified technical, physical, personal and special weakness(es) should be evident in the candidate's answer.

(c) *A good response should include some or most of the points as outlined below.*

### Gathering information on performance strengths or weaknesses

The responses will be relevant to the activity selected but points raised should be justified. Candidates must demonstrate acquired knowledge and understanding in respect of the appropriateness of the method selected.

A link to identified strengths and or weaknesses may be evident. A good response will include reference to whole performance (initial data) and specific (focussed data). To support claims, reference should be made to one or more of the following:
- Movement analysis – observation checklist, match analysis sheet, preparation/action/recovery, time-related observation schedule.
- Mechanical analysis – study of force, balance, centre of gravity etc.
- Consideration of quality – reflection on whether your skill or technique was controlled, fluent, or fast/slow.
- Video – comparison of your performance with that of a model performer. The video allowed playback, freeze frame.
- Coach feedback.
- Fitness testing.

For example, *by looking at my video performance I identified my performance strengths as … I then selected an observation sheet to look more closely at … and so on.*

(d) *A good response should include some or most of the points as outlined below. The candidate's response should include full details, with relevant examples to demonstrate applied knowledge and understanding in how they used this data to construct an improvement plan.*

### Course of action

A good response will include details relevant to the selection and appropriateness of the **most** relevant methods of practice or development or training available. Examples relevant to selected methods and how this will bring about improvement, making the performance more like a model performer, must be evident.

For example, *to make sure my lay-up shot was more like a model performer, I used many repetition drills with no pressure … I then progressed to a practice, which needed more decisions and used combination/conditioned drills to make the shot more effective … Against opposition I was more confident, accurate … and so on.*

### Organising training

Within the response, examples should include: awareness of previously stated strengths and weaknesses; setting of goals and linking to data collected; preparation for competitive events. Training considerations should offer examples based on the complexity of identified weaknesses, stages of learning, complexity of task and so on.

(e) *A good response should include some or most of the points as outlined below. The candidate must explain why it is important to continually monitor their improvement programme.*

### The importance of monitoring and reviewing

A response should suggest the benefits of the purpose of monitoring as an ongoing process. The candidate may provide qualitative or quantitative details of whether the programme is effective/working, and if it supports specific fitness or skill progress. Make reference to using appropriate data collection to allow: comparison of improvements, achieving of set targets; gaining and acting on feedback; aiding motivation and ensuring further progress.

Importantly, the response may include reference to reviewing performance as a summative process. Many candidates will repeat or include some of the previously mentioned comments. However reference to the evaluation of the whole process, that is the impact of the training or development programme, should be highlighted. Judgements on the success or effectiveness of the programme used **plus** judgements on the success or effectiveness to whole performance must be satisfactorily defined.

## PREPARATION OF THE BODY

3. (a) *A good response should include some or most of the points as outlined below. The candidate should select **two** aspects of fitness and explain why each is important to a successful performance.*

### Physical skill-related and mental types of fitness

The candidate should select the most appropriate aspect to show how their relevant knowledge and understanding supports the answer.

**Physical fitness**: cardio respiratory endurance, speed, muscular endurance, flexibility, stamina, strength, speed endurance, power.
**Skill related fitness**: reaction time, agility, co-ordination, balance, timing.
**Mental fitness**: level of arousal, rehearsal, managing emotion.

All responses should suggest how the aspect(s) chosen relate to **effective** performance in the activity.

**Physical fitness**: For example, *in football a high level of cardio respiratory endurance and speed endurance allowed me to track back and help my defence … as well as support the attackers … throughout the whole game … also having good strength as a defender allowed me to jump and challenge for high balls and crosses … and win tackles against the opposition.*
**Skill related fitness**: For example, *in badminton having good agility will allow me quick movement … to reach the shuttle or change direction if necessary and return the shuttle to put my opponent under pressure. Good timing will allow me to hit the shuttle at the correct height above me giving me more chance to win a point because my opponent will struggle to return it.*
**Mental fitness**: For example, *in basketball, as the ball carrier, by managing my emotions I was able to handle the pressure my opponent was putting on me when closely marking … I was able to make the correct decision and carry out the correct pass to my team mate successfully … when taking a free throw, by managing my emotions and rehearsing my routine in my mind I was able to make the free throw successful.*

(b) *A good response should include some or most of the points as outlined below.*

### Accurate collection and recording of data
**Gathering data**: The description of the method could be within or outwith the activity. A diagram may feature in the answer, for example a time-related observation schedule within football that shows information relevant to the particular aspect selected (speed and cardio respiratory endurance). In the answer the candidate may make reference to the process as to how the information was gathered. A narrative account of what was done and **why** should be obvious, showing logical thinking. Methods could include: video performance profiles, stroke/breath/pulse counts and feedback. Reliability and validity of method should be apparent.

Methods could come from outwith the activity or standardised tests may also be described, these could include:
- Physical – 12 minute Cooper test, sit and reach test, Harvard step test, bleep test.
- Skill related – Illinois agility test, ruler drop, alternate hand throw.
- Mental – Questionnaires or self evaluation tests, internal/external feedback.

(c) *A good response should include some or most of the points as outlined below. The candidate must describe a method of training to improve the aspect selected.*

### Appropriate methods of training to improve physical /skill related and mental fitness

The candidates' responses will depend on the choice of activity and the type or aspect of fitness selected. One method of training should be chosen and some candidates may choose one session or a block of time to describe what they did. Training could be within activity/outwith/combination and involve any of the following methods: Fartlek, continuous, conditioning, interval, circuit, weight training, relaxation, breathing and rehearsal.

For example, *I used interval training for swimming … warm up of eight lengths multi stroke … then some stroke improvement … then main set … a 6 × 50 metre swim with a 1minute rest between each set … then sub set … a 6 × 50 metre swim with 45 seconds recovery … This was appropriate because it enables high intensity work combined with rest to allow me to train for a longer period of time and thus gaining greater benefits from training.*

(d) *A good response should include some or most of the points as outlined below. The candidate must demonstrate relevant knowledge and understanding and show critical thinking about how the method of training helped improve their whole performance.*

### Impact on performance

For example, *my Fartlek training helped my whole performance … varied paced running in my sessions … similar to the types of movement in my game of basketball … Fartlek training was exciting and challenging and therefore kept me motivated … now during my basketball game my improved level of CRE … allowed me to keep up with my player even in later stages of the game … I was still able to get back quickly to defend … was able to maintain a high level of performance throughout the game.*
The evidence must relate to the whole performance, with reference to the method of training selected.

(e) *A good response should include some or most of the points as outlined below. The candidate must explain why it is important to continually monitor their performance during training.*

**The monitoring process**

A response will show knowledge about the purpose and importance of the process. It may provide qualitative or quantitative details of whether the training is effective/working. It can support the specific fitness progress. Explanations may include: providing evidence to compare progress; targets; improvements; enabling changes to be made; ensuring future targets; further challenges and promoting motivation. Could also offer whether training method was appropriate; deciding if training was at correct intensity and whether short- or long-term goals had been achieved.

4. (a) *A good response should include some or most of the points as outlined below. The candidate must demonstrate acquired knowledge and understanding in the description of how each type of fitness contributes to effective performance within the selected activity.*

**Physical fitness**: For example, *in badminton CRE is needed to last long rallies and keep my skill level high the whole time. Speed and strength are important to give power so that the smash is difficult to return.*

**Skill-related fitness**: For example, *in badminton having good agility will allow me quick movement ... to reach the shuttle or change direction if necessary and return the shuttle to put my opponent under pressure ... good timing will allow me to hit the shuttle at the correct time, giving me more chance to win a point because my opponent struggles to return it.*

(b) *A good response should include some or most of the points as outlined below. The candidate must demonstrate acquired knowledge and understanding in the description of how mental fitness affects performance within the selected activity.*

**Mental fitness**: For example, *in badminton I need to be able to concentrate for the whole match ... concentrate on each shot ... being focussed ... be determined to win ... not being distracted etc.*

(c) *A good response should include some or most of the points as outlined below. The candidate must describe a training programme used to develop an aspect of fitness.*

A good response should have a description of the form of training for selected approach.

**In the activity (conditioning)**: Fartlek short sprints and then continuous paced running with a description of what they did. For example, *in athletics, for 800 metre running, I did Fartlek training ... did eight laps, jogged the straights and ran the bends ... this was done without stopping ... then did six short 60 metre sprints ... a short 20 metre jog leading into each sprint made the demand similar to end of an actual race.*

**Outwith the activity**: Could include circuit training or weight training with description of what they did sets/reps or types of exercise. For example, *to improve my cardio respiratory endurance for my role as a midfielder in hockey ... I trained outwith the activity ... carried out some circuit training.*

**Combination of both**: Continuous training in pool and weight training out of pool with an appropriate description of each, involving some of the following methods: Fartlek, continuous, conditioning, interval, circuit, weight training, relaxation, breathing or rehearsal.

For example, *in swimming I trained using a combination of training within activity and outwith the activity ... within I used interval training ... did warm up ... then stroke improvement ... main set 6 x 50 metre swim with 1 minute recovery ... subset 6 x 50 with 45 secs recovery ... then warm down. Outwith the pool I did a weight training circuit ... doing a series of exercises ... three sets of exercises ... also some work on stepping machines ... rowing machines ... to improve cardio respiratory endurance* and so on.

The candidate may also refer to the length of the training programme, progressive overload, frequency, intensity, duration, adaptation, rest/recovery, targets they set themselves.

(d) *A good response should include some or most of the points as outlined below.*

**Principles of training**

The answer must refer to the principles of training. Most of the following principles should be referred to: specificity to activity, person and performance, progressive overload, frequency, intensity, duration, adaptation, rest/recovery, over training, reversibility.

You will probably have a description of how they were applied to the programme and also an explanation and justification of why they were considered.

For example, *I made sure the training was specific to the weakness identified ... also demands of activity ... I trained three times per week with rest every other day ... allowed body to recover ... applied overload after week three ... increased number of sets ... training became harder and body adapted to new load ... as I was getting fitter ... variety within programme ... prevent boredom and keep motivation high.*

(e) *The candidate should include next future development needs for either physical, skill related or mental fitness.*

Reference should be made to how this is currently affecting performance and a summary of how they would develop this type of fitness. The candidate should also explain the effects this future development need may have on their performance. For example, *with improved agility I will be able to move and turn quickly when trying to lose my marker and receive a pass.*

**SKILLS AND TECHNIQUES**

5. (a) *A good response should include some or most of the points as outlined below.*

**Gathering information on performance strengths or weaknesses**

The responses will be wide ranging and relevant to the activity selected but points raised should be justified. Candidates must demonstrate acquired knowledge and understanding in respect of the appropriateness of the method selected.

A link to identified strengths and or weaknesses may be evident. A good response will include reference to whole performance (initial data) and be specific in order to support claims. Reference should be made to one or more of the following:

- Movement Analysis - Observation checklist, Match Analysis sheet,
- Mechanical Analysis - Study of force, balance, centre of gravity etc.
- Consideration of Quality - Reflection on whether your skill or technique was controlled, fluent, or fast/slow.
- Video – Comparison of your performance with that of a model performer. *The video allowed playback, freeze frame.*

For example, *by looking at my video performance I identified my performance strengths as ... I then selected an observation sheet to look more closely at ...* and so on.

(b) *A good response should include some or most of the points as outlined below. The responses will be wide ranging and relevant to the activity selected but points raised should be justified. Candidates must demonstrate acquired Knowledge and Understanding relevant to the appropriateness of the method when collecting information on a specific skill.*

## Gathering Information on Performance Strengths or Weaknesses

A link to identified strengths and or weaknesses may be evident. A good response will include reference to specific (focussed data). To support claims reference should be made to one or more of the following:

- Movement analysis – observation checklist, match analysis sheet, preparation/action/ recovery, time-related observation schedule.
- Mechanical analysis – study of force, balance, centre of gravity etc.
- Consideration of quality – reflection on whether your skill or technique was controlled, fluent, or fast/slow.
- Video – comparison of your performance with that of a model performer. *The video allowed playback, freeze frame.*

For example, *by looking at my video performance, I identified the strengths of my skill as … I then selected an observation sheet to look more closely at … and so on.*

(c) *A good response should include some or most of the points as outlined below. Candidate's response should demonstrate knowledge and critical thinking as to why the methods used were appropriate.*

## Appropriate methods of data collection

Explanations offered about appropriateness may include the following: provides evidence to compare progress; targets; aids improvements; is a permanent record; can be used time and time again; aids motivation and ensures further challenge and progress; information can be gathered at the beginning/middle and end and so on. If video is used, reference will be made to pause/rewind facility etc.

(d) *A good response should include some or most of the points as outlined below. The candidate's response should demonstrate a detailed description of an improvement programme.*

## Practice considerations

A good response may include details relevant to the selection and appropriateness of the most relevant methods of practice, development or training available. Considerations of different methods will be evident in the process. Examples relevant to selected methods will be included highlighting the selections made.

- At the cognitive stage – *many shadow or repetition practices were incorporated.*
- At the associative stage – *some shadow or repetition practices, progressing to combination drills.*
- At the automatic stage of learning – *more pressure or problem-solving drills were used to advance and challenge learning and performance development.*

A link to other relevant factors may include: whole part gradual build up, closed/open contexts etc.

## Programme of work

The responses offered will depend on the candidate's choice of skill /technique identified for development. This may include details of the appropriateness of the methods of practice or development programme followed. The programme followed should refer to some of the following considerations: stages of learning, skill complexity, skill classification, model performer, feedback, goal setting and so on.

Programme references may include details of weeks 1 and 2, weeks 3 and 4, weeks 5 and 6, etc. Or, *I used a gradual build up /whole part whole approach to my development programme.* In this respect the notion of reliability and validity should be apparent and justified etc.

The content and structure given must be justified with progressions exemplified to demonstrate sound knowledge and understanding. For example, *as I was at the cognitive stage, I used many shadow and repetition practices to ensure … At the associative stage I used some shadow and repetition practices … At the automatic stage of learning I knew to use more pressure as this would challenge me more … I found the [chosen] skill very difficult so decided to use gradual build up as this would … In weeks 1 and 2 I concentrated more on simple drills … in weeks 3 and 4, I progressed to more complex drills such as … this built my confidence as I reached my target of … and so on.*

A link to other relevant factors may include: whole part, gradual build up, closed/open contexts, repetitions, target setting, model performers etc.

(e) *A good response should include some or most of the points as outlined below.*

## Whole performance development

The responses offered may suggest the impact of improved skill/technique development to **whole** performance effectiveness. For example, a more consistent application, fewer errors, more points won, a positive benefit including greater confidence etc.

The candidate may also include details referencing specific drills or parts of the programme that benefited their performance, for example *I felt that the repetition drills such as … improved my ability to … and so on.*

6. (a) *A good response should include some or most of the points as outlined below. The candidate's response should demonstrate critical thinking when describing the strengths and weaknesses in their performance.*

## Features of a skilled performance

A link to relevant factors may include: a repertoire of skills evident and executed at the correct time with consistency or inconsistency; fluency or non fluency.; movements or application of skills seeming effortless or requiring effort; management of emotions is controlled or uncontrolled; a degree of confidence; few unforced errors; making appropriate decisions when under pressure or poor decisions.

Ability to vary and adapt by using a range of skills and techniques, considering the correct options for the various performance demands.

(b) *A good response should include some or most of the points as outlined below. Candidates should select a skill or techniques and describe **two** methods of practice with examples.*

Methods of practice: Give detailed examples of the methods of practice you have used to develop the skill/technique. For example, shadow practice and combination drill; *for shadow practice I went through the action of the smash without a shuttle. I did this five times and got feedback from my partner.*

(c) *A good response should include some or most of the points as outlined below. The candidate's response should demonstrate sound knowledge and understanding about the effect of these methods of practice on their whole performance.*

## Whole performance development

The responses offered may suggest the impact of improved skill/technique development to **whole** performance effectiveness. For example, a more consistent application, fewer errors, more points won, a positive benefit including greater confidence etc.

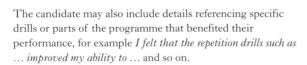

The candidate may also include details referencing specific drills or parts of the programme that benefited their performance, for example *I felt that the repetition drills such as … improved my ability to … and so on.*

Merit will be given to the feasibility, validity and/or justification for claims of improved performance.

(d) *A good response should include some or most of the points as outlined below. The candidate's response should demonstrate sound knowledge and understanding of the principles of effective practice when developing their skill or technique.*

*Principles of effective practice*
Often the acronym **S.M.A.R.T.E.R.** features in a candidate's answers. A good response may include a discussion of each of the principles and how they were applied to the practices. For example, *practice should be specific, measurable, attainable, realistic, time related, exciting and regular. As my programme was specific, it helped me to achieve success … I could target the specific part of my technique that needed most improvement. I knew to set targets and raise them once … this ensured my practice was motivating* etc.

Other relevant knowledge will reference factors such as, *practice needs to show progression to ensure targets were reached. Increased motivation, improved confidence, consideration of work-rest ratio* etc.

(e) *A good response should include some or most of the points as outlined below. The candidate must select either motivation, concentration or feedback and explain its importance in the development of their performance.*

**Motivation/concentration/feedback**
In this respect the candidate may give a synopsis of how one of the factors selected impacted upon their learning and/or their application of skill/technique in the overall performance. Merit should be given according to relevance of explanations offered.

**Motivation**: A good response may include details of being internally/externally motivated to learn or achieve success. Being motivated enables the performer to: be self driven; listen to instruction and act on it; be self determined; give of their best; come from behind; respond to immediate problems or competitive challenges; not worry if mistakes are made and re channel focus.

**Concentration**: A good response may include details of the need to concentrate/focus on instruction or demonstration offered in order to: ensure effective application of skill or technique; promote progression or adaptation of skill or technique; ensure bad habits are not formed; enable the performer to perform their role and apply their skills appropriately.
In the context of games, concentration enables the performer to stick to role-related duties and so on.

**Feedback**: A good response will include details of receiving internal feedback to progress or refine skill/technique; receiving/giving external feedback (visual/verbal/written to progress/refine skill/technique of self or that of others). Feedback should be positive and immediate to promote confidence and/or success.

## STRUCTURES, STRATEGIES AND COMPOSITIONS

7. (a) *A good response should include some or most of the points as outlined below. The candidate must demonstrate applied knowledge and understanding when describing a SSC in detail.*

**Select a relevant structure, strategy or composition**
The candidate must describe the structure, strategy or composition. Some will also make reference to the role they played.
These could include:
- Basketball – fast break, zones, 1–3–1, horseshoe offence, man-to-man defence.
- Football – 4–2–4 or 4–3–3 or 3–5–2.
- Badminton – front and back or sides.
- Gymnastics – particular sequence/routine.
- Volleyball – rotation.
- Hockey – penalty corner.
- Dance – a particular dance or routine used.

For example, *in tennis I used a serve–volley strategy. I would serve fast and hard to opponent, follow my serve, get into net and quickly use a volley to win the point from the opponent's return.*

(b) *A good response should include some or most of the points as outlined below.*

Methods to gather information the effectiveness of the SSC may include video analysis, observation schedules, knowledge of results, personal reflection, internal/external feedback.

(c) *A good response should include some or most of the points as outlined below. The candidate must be able to explain any problem they had when using the SSC.*

**Limitations of various SSC**
The responses will be wide ranging and will depend on the choice of SSC selected. Responses should start with a description of the problems faced, for example *… in basketball my 2–1–2 zone defence can be exposed by my opponents having a strong outside shooter, who could consistently score from outside the key … in my 4–4–2 my opponents played a long ball over the top of our defence, allowing an opportunity … and so on.*

(d) *A good response should include some or most of the points as outlined below. The candidate must demonstrate relevant critical thinking and decision making to explain the actions they took to improve the effectiveness of their performance.*

**The importance of adapting and refining a structure, strategy or composition in response to performance demands**
The responses will depend on the choice of structure, strategy or composition selected. Responses could start with a brief description of the problem faced, then show evidence of problem solving and decision making to make their performance more effective. The candidate may decide to change structure, strategy or composition completely. For example, *in basketball we were playing a 2–1–2 zone … opposition had good outside shooters … scored frequently … we changed to half court man-to-man defence to stop them … we picked up our players at the half court … always made sure we were basket side … marked tightly when they attempted to shoot this led to fewer successful shots as they were under more pressure …. forced them to try and drive to basket. They made more mistakes … scored fewer baskets as they were poor at driving to basket … we won more turnovers and could attack more.*

(e) *A good response should include some or most of the points as outlined below*

**Using information on team/individual performance to make appropriate decisions when developing, and monitoring performance**
Information may come from before performance, for example previous *knowledge of weather or playing surface.* It may come from during the performance, for example time and score. This would then be used to plan and develop performance by processing the information and taking decisions to develop performance.

**8.** (a) *A good response should include some or most of the points as outlined below.*

### Roles and relationships

Discuss individual strengths and weaknesses in a structure, strategy or composition. For example, *in tennis I used a serve–volley strategy. I would serve fast and hard to opponent, follow my serve, get into net and quickly use a volley to win the point from the opponent's return. My strengths were I had a consistent and fast first serve, a high percentage of being in etc.*

### Recognising the demands of individual roles during performance

For example, *in basketball, as a centre, my role in my 2–1–2 zone was to block out and rebound in defence … and so on.*

(b) *A good response should include some or most of the points as outlined below.*

Candidates must relate to their specific role within the SSC and describe a weakness. For example, *as a centre I was unable to block out and collect the rebound, as I was unable to hold players out and jump with power to collect rebounds.* **Or**, *my role within our dance performance was to shadow the movements of my partner, however I was unable to complete some of the more difficult motifs.*

(c) *A good response should include some or most of the points as outlined below.*

Candidates should respond by explaining the effects the weakness had on their whole performance. For example, *as I was unable to collect the rebound, this meant that my opponent could score an easy basket.* **Or**, *as I was unable to carry out more complex motifs, it resulted in our performance being out of time and not … and so on.*

(d) *A good response should include some or most of the points as outlined below.*

### Programme of work

They will describe a programme of work, taking cognisance of weaknesses described previously: a range of programmes may be offered including practising parts in isolation and unopposed/opposed practices/games. The content and structure must be justified, with possible progressions within programme to explain the actions.
Candidates may also change or adopt the SSC either as individuals or as a team as a short-term measure.

(e) *A good response should include some or most of the points as outlined below*

### Monitoring

Methods to evaluate the effectiveness of the SSC video analysis, observation schedules, knowledge of results, personal reflection, internal/external feedback.
Comparisons to previous games may also be included.

## INTERMEDIATE 2 PHYSICAL EDUCATION 2010

In relation to **all** questions it should be noted that the relevance of the content in the candidates' responses will depend on:

- the activity selected
- the performance focus
- the training/development programme/programme of work selected
- the practical experiences of their course as the contexts for answers.

### PERFORMANCE APPRECIATION

**1.** (a) *A good response should include some or most of the points as outlined below. To demonstrate acquired knowledge and understanding, the candidate's must describe a model performance in that activity.*

### Model performance comparison

A good response will include reference to the range and qualities that are evident in a model performer's repertoire. Reference may be made across the range of demands required in performance – technical, physical, skill and mental related.

(b) *A good response should include some or most of the points as outlined below. The candidate's response should include what their weaknesses are compared to a model performance.*

A good response will include reference to the range and qualities that are evident in the model performance repertoire. Reference may be made across the range of demands required in performance – technical, physical, skill and mental related.

In relation to the demand, selected relevant points may come from both the 'like/unlike' perspectives. For example, *unlike a model performer I only have a few skills, I can't hit the shuttle at the correct time and lack consistency and/or fluency; unlike the model performer I look clumsy, they make everything look so easy, their movements and skills are used at the right time.*

(c) *A good response should include some or most of the points as outlined below. The candidate should demonstrate knowledge and understanding of how their performance is affected by mental factors.*

### Mental factors

Candidates may demonstrate acquired knowledge and understanding in the following: the ability to manage emotions, level of arousal (over or under). Handling stress affected by self confidence, motivation/concentration and so on.
The candidate may offer suggestions about the influences on performance being positive and/or negative.

(d) *A good response should include some or most of the points as outlined below. The candidate's response should include detailed discussion to demonstrate what they have done in training to make their performance more like that of a model performance. Specific examples should be given.*

### Course of action

A good response will include details relevant to the selection and appropriateness of the **most** relevant methods of practice/development/training available. Examples relevant to selected methods and how this will bring about improvement more commensurate to model performer must be evident.

For example, *to make sure my lay-up shot was more like a model performer, at first I used many repetition drills in a closed environment to ensure I had no pressure ... I then progressed to more open practice and used combination/conditioned drills to ensure refinement of shot, i.e. against opposition I was more efficient and accurate ... and so on.*

(e) *A good response should include some or most of the points as outlined below*

### Course effectiveness / impact on performance development

A good response **must** include evaluative comments and offer examples on how and why they thought the course of action taken was effective. The candidate could state what the impact of skill/technique development to whole performance development was. For example, *a more consistent shooter with higher shooting average, more points won, a positive benefit including greater confidence/better help to team ... and so on.*

2. (a) *A good response should include some or most of the points as outlined below. The candidate's response should include full details with relevant examples to demonstrate acquired knowledge and understanding of the demands of a quality performance.*

### Nature and demands

**Nature**: Individual/team. The duration of the game/event. The number of player(s)/ performers involved. A spectator/audience event. Indoor/outdoor. Directly/indirectly competitive. Objective /subjective scoring systems in application. Codes of conduct.
**Challenges**: Technical, physical, mental and special.

Candidates may demonstrate acquired knowledge and understanding across all related demands or focus on one more comprehensively. Similarly, candidates may demonstrate acquired knowledge and understanding in respect of the unique game/event challenges or emphasise the challenges unique to the role/solo/duo performance relative to the activity selected.

### Special performance qualities

The responses will be wide ranging and relevant to the activity selected. Candidates may demonstrate acquired knowledge and understanding in respect of the specific role/solo related demands necessary for an effective performance.

(b) *A good response should include some or most of the points as outlined below. The candidate should describe in detail **one** method they have used to gather data about their performance.*

### Gathering information on performance strengths or weaknesses

A link to identified strengths and or weaknesses may be evident. A good response will include reference to whole performance (initial data) and specific (focussed data). To support claims, reference should be made to one or more of the following:
- Movement analysis – observation checklist, match analysis sheet, preparation/action/ recovery/ time-related observation schedule.
- Mechanical analysis – study of force, balance, centre of gravity etc.
- Consideration of quality – reflection on whether your skill or technique was controlled, fluent, or fast/slow.
- Video – comparison of your performance with that of a model performer. *The video allowed playback, freeze frame.*

- Questionnaire – questions should be relevant and have responses such as 'done well', 'needs improvement' or you can mark your performance on a graded scale.
- Coach/observer feedback.

(c) *A good response should include some or most of the points as outlined below. The candidate's response should demonstrate applied knowledge and understanding to how they used the data gathered to plan their training programme.*

### Organising training
Within the response examples should include:
- identifying strengths and weaknesses
- setting of targets
- decisions taken as a result of the performance weaknesses/strengths reflective of appropriate training/development method(s) and/or selected training regimes.

(d) *A good response should include some or most of the points as outlined below.*

### Setting goals
A response will suggest the importance of setting short-term goals to help reach longer-term goals. Examples should be offered to show understanding about how performance gains as a result of setting realistic/attainable goals. For example, *it motivates you to do better ... lets you see if training is working or needs to be progressed. Lets me compare 'before and after' ... is a form of feedback ... establishes achievement ... can be used to judge performance against checklists or model performer and so on.*

Candidates must give examples of the short- and long-term goals.

(e) *A good response should include some or most of the points as outlined below. The candidate should be able to show **acquired knowledge**.*

### Monitoring training using particular methods
Methods used could include: video, observation schedules, training diary, logbook, personal evaluation or game/performance analysis.

## PREPARATION OF THE BODY

3. (a) *A good response should include some or most of the points as outlined below. The candidate must demonstrate acquired knowledge and understanding through describing in detail the fitness demands for their chosen activity.*

### Activity-specific fitness
A good response should include reference to the activity selected and be able to show both acquired and applied knowledge of the activity specific fitness requirements. Suggestions may be made about the types of fitness – physical, skill related and mental.
**Physical fitness**: For example, *in badminton CRE is needed to last long rallies and keep my skill level high the whole time ... Speed and strength are important to give power so that the smash is difficult to return.*
**Skill-related fitness**: For example, *in badminton, having good agility will allow me quick movement ... to reach the shuttle or change direction if necessary and return the shuttle to put my opponent under pressure ... good timing will allow me to hit the shuttle to the correct place, giving me more chance to win a point because my opponent struggles to return it.*
**Mental fitness**: For example, *in badminton, I need to be able to concentrate for the whole match ... concentrate on each shot ... being focussed ... be determined to win ... not be distracted etc.*

The response may highlight one particular type of fitness but be able to show how the particular aspects within that type are important to the activity. For example, *in basketball physical fitness is important … cardio respiratory endurance is needed … to be able to get up the court quickly to attack … get back and defend… when we lose the ball … power is important to … jump to rebound the ball … in offence and defence … strength is also important to block out opponents on rebounds.*

(b) *A good response should include some or most of the points as outlined below. The candidate must select an aspect of fitness and describe how they assessed their level of fitness.*

### Accurate collection and recording of data

**Gathering data**: The description of the method could be within or outwith the activity. A diagram may feature in the answer, for example a time-related observation schedule within football that shows information relevant to the particular aspect selected (speed and cardio respiratory endurance). In the answer the candidate may make reference to the process as to how the information was gathered. A narrative account of what was done and **why** should be obvious, showing logical thinking. Methods could include: video performance profiles, stroke/breath/pulse counts and feedback.

Methods could come from outwith the activity or standardised tests may also be described, these could include:

- Physical – 12 minute Cooper test, sit and reach test, Harvard step test, bleep test.
- Skill related – Illinois agility test, ruler drop, alternate hand throw.
- Mental – Questionnaires or self evaluation tests, internal/external feedback.

(c) *A good response should include some or most of the points as outlined below. The candidate must demonstrate both acquired and applied knowledge in discussing how the aspect of fitness selected affected their performance.*

**Physical fitness**: Cardio respiratory endurance, speed, muscular endurance, flexibility, stamina, strength, speed endurance, power.
**Skill-related fitness**: Reaction time, agility, co-ordination, balance, timing.
**Mental fitness**: Level of arousal, rehearsal, managing emotion.

All responses should suggest how the aspect chosen affects performance in the activity. They may respond in a positively or negatively

**Physical fitness**: For example, *in football a high level of cardio respiratory endurance and speed endurance allowed me to track back and help my defence … as well as support the attackers … throughout the whole game … also having good strength as a defender allowed me to jump and challenge for high balls and crosses … and win tackles against the opposition.*
**Skill-related fitness**: For example, *in badminton having good agility will allow me quick movement … to reach the shuttle or change direction if necessary and return the shuttle to put my opponent under pressure. Good timing will allow me to hit the shuttle at the correct height above me giving me more chance to win a point because my opponent will struggle to return it.*
**Mental fitness**: For example, *in basketball, as the ball carrier, by managing my emotions I was able to handle the pressure my opponent was putting on me when closely marking … I was able to make the correct decision and carry out the correct pass to my team mate successfully … when taking a free throw, by managing my emotions and rehearsing my routine in my mind I was able to make the free throw successful.*

(d) *A good response should include some or most of the points as outlined below. The candidate must select an appropriate method of training and describe what they did.*

### Appropriate methods of training to improve physical skill related and mental fitness

The candidates' responses will depend on the choice of activity and aspect of fitness selected. Various methods of training could be chosen and some candidates may choose one session or a block of time to describe what they did. If the question asks for information on a session then care should be taken to ensure that the answer is on **a** session – not a programme of work. Training could be within activity/outwith/combination and involve some of the following methods: Fartlek, continuous, conditioning, interval, circuit, weight training, relaxation, breathing and rehearsal.

For example, *I used interval training for swimming … warm up of eight lengths multi stroke … then some stroke improvement … then main set … a 6 × 50 metre swim with a 1 minute rest between each set … then sub set … a 6 × 50 metre swim with 45 seconds recovery … This was appropriate because it enables high intensity work combined with rest to allow me to train for a longer period of time and thus gaining greater benefits from training.*

(e) *A good response should include some or most of the points as outlined below.*

### Impact on performance

For example, *during my basketball game my improved level of CRE … allowed me to keep up with my player even in later stages of the game … I was still able to get back quickly to defend … was able to maintain a high level of performance throughout the game.*
The evidence must relate to the whole performance, with relevant answers given.

4. (a) *A good response should include some or most of the points as outlined below. The candidate should select **one** type of fitness and describe how this type of fitness helped them perform successfully.*

### Activity specific fitness

A good response should include reference to the activity selected and be able to show both acquired and applied knowledge of the activity specific fitness requirements. Suggestions may be made about the types of fitness – physical, skill-related and mental. All responses should suggest how the type chosen relates to successful performance in the activity.
Each type may be broken into a number of aspects of fitness.

**Physical fitness**: For example, *in badminton **CRE** is needed to last long rallies and keep my skill level high the whole time …*

**Skill-related fitness**: For example, *in badminton, having good **agility** will allow me quick movement … to reach the shuttle or change direction if necessary and return the shuttle to put my opponent under pressure …*
**Mental fitness**: For example, *in badminton, I need to be able to **concentrate** for the whole match … concentrate on each shot … being focussed … be determined to win … not be distracted etc.*

(b) *A good response should include some or most of the points as outlined below. The candidate should select one type of fitness which was a weakness and describe how their performance is affected by low levels of this type fitness. Each type may be broken into a number of aspects of fitness.*

**Physical fitness**: For example, *in football a low level of cardio respiratory endurance and speed endurance made me unable to* *track back and help my defence ... as well as being unable to support the attackers... throughout the whole game... also as I had poor strength as a defender I was never able to jump and challenge for high balls and crosses... and win tackles against the opposition.*

**Skill-related fitness**: For example, *in badminton, as I have poor agility I was unable to move quickly and reach the shuttle or change direction if necessary and return the shuttle to put my opponent under pressure. My poor timing did not allow me to hit the shuttle at the correct height above me, giving me less chance to win a point.*

**Mental fitness**: For example, *in basketball I was unable to manage my emotions: I was unable to handle the pressure my opponent was putting on me when he was closely marking me.*

(c) *A good response should include some or most of the points as outlined below. The candidate must demonstrate both acquired and applied knowledge and understanding when considering what principles of training they used when planning a training programme.*

### Principles of training

The answer must refer to the principles of training. Most of the following principles should be referred to: specificity to activity, person and performance, progressive overload, frequency, intensity, duration, adaptation, rest/recovery, over training, reversibility.
The candidate should only give a description of the principles of training considered.

(d) *A good response should include some or most of the points as outlined below. The candidate must demonstrate both acquired and applied knowledge and understanding when applying the principles of training to their training programme.*

Candidates should describe how they were applied to the programme and also explain and justify why they were considered.
For example, *I made sure the training was specific to the weakness identified ... also demands of activity ... I trained three times per week with rest every other day ... allowed body to recover ... applied overload after week three ... increased number of sets ... training became harder and body adapted to new load ... as I was getting fitter ... variety within programme ... prevent boredom and keep motivation high.*

(e) *A good response should include some or most of the points as outlined below*

### The monitoring process

A response will show knowledge about the purpose and importance of the process. It may provide qualitative or quantitative details of whether the training is effective/working. It can support the specific fitness progress. Explanations may include: providing evidence to compare progress; targets; improvements; enabling changes to be made; ensuring future targets; further challenges and promote motivation. Also whether the training method was appropriate, deciding if training was at correct intensity and whether short-term or long-term goals have been achieved.

## SKILLS AND TECHNIQUES

5. (a) *A good response should include some or most of the points as outlined below. The candidate's response should demonstrate acquired knowledge and understanding when describing a model performance of their selected skill or technique.*

### Features of a skilled performance
A good response will include references to the range of qualities involved when describing a model performance of the skill. A link to other relevant factors such as breaking the skill down into preparation, action, recovery, execution

with the correct time, with consistency, fluency, eases of economy; movements/application of skill seem effortless when performing.

### Skill classification
Provide a relevant description of various types of skill. The description should include details appropriate to the skills selected inclusive of example. The classified skills likely to appear are: open/closed and simple/complex.

Candidates may decide to break down the skill to preparation/action/recovery and describe the skill or technique using these sub-headings. They may also make reference to the consistency, fluency, timing, etc. Movements or application of skills seem effortless; management of emotions is controlled; degree of confidence; few unforced errors; makes appropriate decisions when under pressure.

(b) *A good response should include some or most of the points as outlined below. The candidate should describe how they gathered information on their selected skill or technique.*

### Gathering information on performance strengths or weaknesses
The responses will be wide ranging and relevant to the activity selected but points raised should be justified. Candidates must demonstrate acquired knowledge and understanding in respect of the appropriateness of the method selected.

A link to identified strengths and or weaknesses may be evident. A good response will include reference to whole performance (initial data) and specific (focussed data). To support claims reference should be made to one or more of the following:
- Movement analysis – observation checklist, match analysis sheet, preparation/action/ recovery, time-related observation schedule.
- Mechanical analysis – study of force, balance, centre of gravity etc.
- Consideration of quality – reflection on whether your skill or technique was controlled, fluent, or fast/slow.
- Video – comparison of your performance with that of a model performer. *The video allowed playback, freeze frame.*

*For example, by looking at my video performance I identified my performance strengths as ... I then selected an observation sheet to look more closely at ... and so on.*

(c) *A good response should include some or most of the points as outlined below. The candidate's response should demonstrate critical thinking when discussing why the methods were appropriate.*

### Appropriate methods of data collection
Description of the method(s) used must be offered; a diagram may feature to support the answer. The appropriateness of the methods described should enable either qualitative or quantitative details of performance progress. A range of relevant methods will be selected from movement, mechanical analysis or consideration of quality.

Explanations offered about appropriateness may include the following: provides evidence to compare progress; targets; aids improvements; is a permanent record; can be used time and time again; aids motivation and ensures further challenge and progress; information can be gathered at the beginning/middle and end and so on. If video is used, reference will be made to pause/rewind facility etc.

(d) *A good response should include some or most of the points as outlined below. The candidate's response should describe in detail the programme of work used.*

### Programme of work

The responses offered will depend on the candidate's choice of skill /technique identified for development. This may include details of the appropriateness of the methods of practice or development programme followed. The programme followed should refer to some of the following considerations: stages of learning, skill complexity, skill classification, model performer, feedback, goal setting and so on.

Programme references may include details of weeks 1 and 2, weeks 3 and 4, weeks 5 and 6, etc. **Or,** *I used a gradual build up /whole part whole approach to my development programme.* In this respect the notion of reliability and validity should be apparent and justified etc.

The content and structure given must be justified with progressions exemplified to demonstrate sound knowledge and understanding. For example, *as I was at the cognitive stage, I used many shadow and repetition practices to ensure … At the associative stage I used some shadow and repetition practices … At the automatic stage of learning I knew to use more pressure as this would challenge me more … I found the* [chosen] *skill very difficult so decided to use gradual build up as this would … In weeks 1 and 2 I concentrated more on simple drills … in weeks 3 and 4, I progressed to more complex drills such as … this built my confidence as I reached my target of …* and so on.

A link to other relevant factors may include: whole part, gradual build up, closed/open contexts, repetitions, target setting, model performers etc.

(e) *A good response should include some or most of the points as outlined below.*

### The use of model performance

A good response will include reference to the appropriateness of model performance, when developing their personal improvement plan. Most likely this will relate to skill learning or development. For example, using a model performer can advantage performance in a number of ways:

- Identify strengths and weaknesses.
- Increase confidence and/or motivation.
- Provide various types of feedback.
- Provide challenge in practice or competition.
- Provide accurate feeds continuously.
- Inspire to achieve higher levels of achievement.
- Support planning practice/targets.
- Inspire to copy ideas.

6. (a) *A good response should include some or most of the points as outlined below. The candidate should describe how they gathered information on their selected skill or technique.*

### Appropriate methods of data collection

Description of the method(s) used must be offered; a diagram could be used to support the answer. The appropriateness of the methods described should enable either qualitative or quantitative details of performance progress. A range of relevant methods will be selected from movement, mechanical analysis or consideration of quality.

Reference should be made to one or more of the following:

- Movement analysis – observation checklist, match analysis sheet, preparation/action/recovery.
- Mechanical analysis – study of force, balance, centre of gravity etc.
- Consideration of quality – reflection on whether your skill or technique was controlled, fluent, or fast/slow.
- Video – comparison of your performance with that of a model performer. The video allowed playback, freeze frame.

(b) *A good response should include some or most of the points as outlined below. The candidate's response should demonstrate critical thinking to how they used this information to plan an appropriate programme of work.*

### Analysis of the data gathered

A link to identified weaknesses should be evident. A good response will include reference to whole performance and these will be linked to the programme of work planned/used. For example, *by looking at my video performance I identified my performance weaknesses were … I then decided that I should focus on my smash … the programme or work would be specific to my weakness.*

(c) *A good response should include some or most of the points as outlined below. The candidate's response should demonstrate knowledge and understanding to how they ensure that the practices they used were effective.*

### Principles of effective practice

Often the acronym **S.M.A.R.T.E.R.** features in a candidate's answers. A good response may include a discussion of each of the principles and how they were applied to the practices. For example, *practice should be specific, measurable, attainable, realistic, time related, exciting and regular. As my programme was specific, it helped me to achieve success … I could target the specific part of my technique that needed most improvement. I knew to set targets and raise them once … this ensured my practice was motivating* etc.

Other relevant knowledge will reference factors such as, *practice needs to show progression to ensure targets were reached. Increased motivation, improved confidence, consideration of work-rest ratio* etc.

(d) *A good response should include some or most of the points as outlined below.*

### Monitoring and review

Reference to appropriate data methods to facilitate comparison of improvements. Many candidates will repeat or include some of the previously mentioned, such as focused observation schedule, keeping a diary.

(e) *A good response should include some or most of the points as outlined below.*

The candidate should identify a future development need from which to further improve their performance. A good response will show how they identified this future development need, what specific difficulties they had and a summary of how they intended to work on this. The candidate should also describe the effect this may have on their performance.

## STRUCTURES, STRATEGIES AND COMPOSITIONS

7. (a) *A good response should include some or most of the points as outlined below. The candidate must demonstrate acquired knowledge and understanding regarding structure, strategy or composition selected and be able to describe in detail.*

### Select a relevant structure, strategy or composition

The candidate must describe the structure, strategy or composition. Some will also make reference to the role they played.
These could include:

- Basketball – fast break, zones, 1–3–1, horseshoe offence, man-to-man defence.
- Football – 4–2–4 or 4–3–3 or 3–5–2.
- Badminton – front and back or sides.
- Gymnastics – particular sequence/routine.
- Volleyball – rotation.
- Hockey – penalty corner.

• Dance – a particular dance or routine used.

For example, *in tennis I used a serve–volley strategy. I would serve fast and hard to opponent, follow my serve, get into net and quickly use a volley to win the point from the opponent's return.*

(b) *A good response should include some or most of the points as outlined below. The candidate must demonstrate how the selected element was a strength in their SSC.*

#### Structure and strategy fundamentals

The following may be referred to or listed: using space in attack and defence; tempo of play; speed in attack; delay in defence and principles of play (width; depth and mobility). The importance should be justified and show both acquired and applied knowledge.

For example, *in basketball I wanted to play a fast tempo game … attack quickly … so I made sure that on each opportunity we tried to play a fast break … to catch the defence out … score a quick basket … create an overload situation … before the defence was organised properly.*

#### Structure and compositional fundamentals

The following may be referred to or listed: design form – developing motifs; linking movements; using space effectively. The importance discussed should show both acquired and applied knowledge.

For example, *in dance I started with a simple step motif … took me forwards then back to starting position … then sideways … back to starting … I established this as a simple core motif … then I developed a second core motif … this time a jumping pattern … then I began to mix and play with both core motifs … to add interest to my dance … gave my dance variety and quality of movement contrasts.*

(c) *A good response should include some or most of the points as outlined below. The candidate must demonstrate how the selected element (must be **different**) was a **weakness in** their SSC.*

#### Structure and strategy fundamentals

The following may be referred to or listed: using space in attack and defence; tempo of play; speed in attack; delay in defence and principles of play (width; depth and mobility). The weakness should be justified and show both acquired and applied knowledge.

For example, *in netball our goal attack was unable to create space, as she was unable to lose her marker.*

#### Structure and compositional fundamentals

The following may be referred to or listed: design form; developing motifs; using repetition; variation and contrast; using space effectively; using creativity in performance. The weakness discussed should show both acquired and applied knowledge.

For example, *in trampolining, as I was unable to carry out more complex skills, my performance lacked variation and therefore I did not achieve a high mark.*

(d) *A good response should include some or most of the points as outlined below. The candidate must demonstrate relevant critical thinking when describing the decisions they took to improve the effectiveness of their SSC.*

#### The importance of adapting and refining a structure, strategy or composition in response to performance demands

The responses will depend on the choice of structure, strategy or composition selected. Responses could start with a brief description of the problem faced, then show evidence of problem solving and decision making to make their performance more effective. The candidate may decide to change structure, strategy or composition completely. For

example, *in basketball we were playing a 2–1–2 zone … opposition had good outside shooters … scored frequently … we changed to half court man-to-man defence to stop them.*

(e) *A good response should include some or most of the points as outlined below.*

Responses should show how the decisions selected in part (*d*) have affected the whole performance.

For example, *in basketball this led to fewer successful shots as they were under more pressure …. forced them to try and drive to basket. They made more mistakes … scored fewer baskets as they were poor at driving to basket … we won more turnovers and could attack more.*

8. (a) *A good response should include some or most of the points as outlined below. The candidate must demonstrate applied knowledge and understanding when describing their **role/performance** in the SSC.*

#### Select a relevant structure, strategy or composition

The candidate must describe the structure, strategy or composition. Some will also make reference to the role they played.
These could include:

• Basketball – fast break, zones, 1–3–1, horseshoe offence, man-to-man defence.
• Football – 4–2–4 or 4–3–3 or 3–5–2.
• Badminton – front and back or sides.
• Gymnastics – particular sequence/routine.
• Volleyball – rotation.
• Hockey – penalty corner.
• Dance – a particular dance or routine used.

For example, *in tennis I used a serve–volley strategy. I would serve fast and hard to opponent, follow my serve, get into net and quickly use a volley to win the point from the opponent's return.*

#### Recognising the demands of individual roles during performance

For example, *in basketball, as a centre, my role was to rebound the ball in offence and block out in defence etc.*

The candidate must describe their role/performance in the SSC.

(b) *A good response should include some or most of the points as outlined below. The candidate must demonstrate applied knowledge and understanding about how they gathered information on their **role/performance** within the SSC.*

#### Data collection on role/performance

Description of the method(s) used must be offered a diagram may feature to support the answer. A range of relevant methods will be selected, such as an observation schedule, coach feedback and/or video footage. Information relevant to the particular aspects of the structure, strategy or composition will be evident.

(c) *A good response should include some or most of the points as outlined below.*

#### Roles and relationships

#### Individual strengths and weaknesses in a structure, strategy or composition

For example, *in tennis I used a serve–volley strategy. I would serve fast and hard to opponent, follow my serve, get into net and position and quickly use a volley to win the point from the opponent's return, however I was not quick enough to get into the correct position to execute a winning volley.*

(d) *A good response should include some or most of the points as outlined below. The candidate must describe the actions they took to address the weakness(es) identified.*

**The importance of adapting and refining a structure, strategy or composition in response to performance demands**

The responses will depend on the choice of structure, strategy or composition selected. Responses could start with a brief description of the problem faced, then show evidence of problem solving and decision making to make their performance more effective. The candidate may decide to change structure, strategy or composition completely. For example, *in basketball we were playing a 2–1–2 zone ... opposition had good outside shooters ... scored frequently ... we changed to half court man-to-man defence to stop them ...this led to less successful shots as they were under more pressure ... forced them to try and drive to basket. They made more mistakes ... scored fewer baskets as they were poor at driving to basket ... we won more turnovers and could attack more.*

The candidate may also decide to complete a training programme to address weaknesses.

(*e*) *A good response should include some or most of the points as outlined below.*

### Effect on whole performance

For example, *in football we played a 4–4–2 formation ... we found when attacking that all four players in midfield would be up the park ... supporting the forwards ... when the attack broke down the opposition often broke quickly ... our midfield were slow to get back ... our defence was under pressure ... we adapted the structure, strategy or composition by having one player ... holding in midfield in front of back four ... one midfield supporting strikers ... and two in the middle to move back and forward as necessary ... this led to a more balanced attack and defence and allowed us to prevent the opposition breaking quickly ... holding midfielder was able to delay attack ... allow others to get back ... and so on.*

# INTERMEDIATE 2 PHYSICAL EDUCATION 2011

In relation to **all** questions it should be noted that the relevance of the content in the candidates' responses will depend on:

- the activity selected
- the performance focus
- the training/development programme/programme of work selected
- the practical experiences of their course as the contexts for answers.

## PERFORMANCE APPRECIATION

1. (*a*) **Qualities**

In relation to any of the qualities selected a description should be offered of a quality performance.
Candidates may demonstrate acquired Knowledge and Understanding in respect of:
**Technical Qualities:** Reference may be made to a repertoire of skills eg *dribbling, passing shooting etc* is consistent and accurate. This may be accompanied by clarification of success rate or quality of execution or PAR. Reference may also be made to the classification of skills demanded, eg simple/complex etc.
**Physical Qualities:** Candidates may opt to use steers or not. Examples are given below of possible responses;
eg *in my gymnastics routine I used a strong, powerful round off going down the mats and on the way back I used light, springy jumps. Or high levels of Cardio Respiratory Endurance, Speed Endurance helped maintain pace and track my opponents continuously...*

**Personal Qualities:** Reference may be made to inherent qualities, eg *qualities such as being determined or confident or competitive... etc, helped because opponents felt threatened...*
**Special Qualities:** Reference may be made to the ability to create opportunity, deceive opponents, make performance look more dynamic, apply flair, had the ability to choreograph routines, link skills ....etc.
eg *These unique qualities helped to fake intent and so wrong foot opponent. The routine was exciting to watch. This helped gain more points* etc.

(*b*) **Qualities**

In relation to any of the qualities selected a description should be offered of a quality performance.
Candidates may demonstrate acquired Knowledge and Understanding in respect of:
**Technical Qualities:** Reference may be made to a repertoire of skills eg *dribbling, passing shooting etc* is consistent and accurate. This may be accompanied by clarification of success rate or quality of execution or PAR. Reference may also be made to the classification of skills demanded, eg simple/complex etc.
**Physical Qualities:** Candidates may opt to use steers or not. Examples are given below of possible responses;
eg *in my gymnastics routine I used a strong, powerful round off going down the mats and on the way back I used light, springy jumps. Or high levels of Cardio Respiratory Endurance, Speed Endurance helped maintain pace and track my opponents continuously...*
**Personal Qualities:** Reference may be made to inherent qualities, eg *qualities such as being determined or confident or competitive... etc, helped because opponents felt threatened...*
**Special Qualities:** Reference may be made to the ability to create opportunity, deceive opponents, make performance look more dynamic, apply flair, had the ability to choreograph routines, link skills ...etc.

Eg *These unique qualities helped to fake intent and so wrong foot opponent. The routine was exciting to watch. This helped gain more points* etc.

### (c) Setting goals

A response will give examples of specific goals set. Eg *I decided to set myself a short term goal of increasing my power. My long term goal would be to use this effectively when spiking in Volleyball.*

### (d) Course of action

A good response will include details relevant to the selection and appropriateness of the **MOST** relevant methods of practice/development ie training available. Examples relevant to selected methods and how this will bring about improvement more commensurate to model performer must be evident.

For example, *to make sure my lay up shot was more like a model performer. At first I used many repetition drills in a closed environment to ensure I had no pressure... etc.
I then progressed to more open practice and used combinations ie conditioned drills to ensure refinement of shot ie against opposition I was more efficient, accurate...*

### (e) Course effectiveness/impact on performance development

A satisfactory candidate response MUST include evaluative comments and offer examples on how and why they thought the course of action taken was effective. Eg the candidate could state what the impact of skill/technique development to WHOLE performance development was. For example, a more consistent shooter with higher shooting average/more points won, a positive benefit including greater confidence ie better help to team etc.

## 2. (a) Qualities

In relation to any of the qualities selected a description should be offered of a quality performance.
Candidates may demonstrate acquired Knowledge and Understanding in respect of:

**Technical Qualities:** Reference may be made to a repertoire of skills eg *dribbling, passing shooting etc is consistent and accurate.* This may be accompanied by clarification of success rate or quality of execution or PAR. Reference may also be made to the classification of skills demanded, eg simple/complex etc.

**Physical Qualities:** Candidates may opt to use steers or not. Examples are given below of possible responses; eg *in my gymnastics routine I used a strong, powerful round off going down the mats and on the way back I used light, springy jumps. Or high levels of Cardio Respiratory Endurance, Speed Endurance helped maintain pace and track my opponents continuously...*

**Personal Qualities:** Reference may be made to inherent qualities, eg *qualities such as being determined or confident or competitive... etc, helped because opponents felt threatened...*

**Special Qualities:** Reference may be made to the ability to create opportunity, deceive opponents, make performance look more dynamic, apply flair, had the ability to choreograph routines, link skills ....etc.
Eg *These unique qualities helped to fake intent and so wrong foot opponents...The routine was exciting to watch...This helped gain more points* etc.

### (b) Gathering Information on Performance Strengths or Weaknesses

A link to identified strengths and or weaknesses may be evident. A satisfactory response will include reference to whole performance (initial data) and specific (focused data). To substantiate claims reference should be made to one or more of the following:

- Movement Analysis (Observation checklist, Match Analysis sheet).
- Preparation/Action/Recovery: Mechanical Analysis of force, levers, propulsion etc
- Consideration of Quality: reflecting on whether your skill or technique was controlled/fluent, or fast/slow?
- Video – Comparison of your performance with that of a model performer. The video allowed playback, freeze frame.
- Questionnaire: Questions should be relevant to and have responses such as 'done well', 'needs improvement' or mark your performance on a graded scale.

### (c) Strengths and Weaknesses

The responses will be relevant to the activity selected. Candidates may demonstrate acquired Knowledge and Understanding in respect of the specific role or team/solo responsibilities, strengths & weaknesses. Most likely a relevant analysis in relation to the identified technical, physical, personal and special strengths & weaknesses may be evident in the candidates' answer.

### (d) Planning implications

The candidate's experiences will dictate the terms of reference used, eg From an individual/team game performer's; an athlete's or swimmer's perspective some of the following training terms will most commonly be used: short/long term targets; pre-season; competitive season and post season; to train in/out with the activity.
A satisfactory response will consider both acquired and applied Knowledge and Understanding. In this respect, the link to their identified needs will be highlighted with examples from the particular stages of training and types of training used. To ensure training effectiveness related Knowledge and Understanding about training principles or principles of effective practice will most likely be made.

### (e) Monitoring

Importantly, the response may include reference to reviewing performance = summative process. Many candidates may repeat or include some of the previously mentioned methods.

## PREPARATION OF THE BODY

**3. (a) Physical fitness** – eg *in badminton CRE is needed to last long rallies and keep my skill level high the whole time... Speed and strength are important to give power so that the smash is difficult to return.*

**Skill related fitness** – eg *in badminton having good agility will allow me quick movement...; to reach the shuttle or change direction if necessary and return the shuttle to put my opponent under pressure-also...; good timing will allow me to hit the shuttle at the correct place giving me more chance to win a point because my opponent struggles to return it.*

**Mental fitness** – eg *in badminton I need to be able to concentrate for the whole match...; concentrate on each shot...; being focussed...; be determined to win...; not being distracted etc.*

### (b) Accurate collection and recording of data
### Gathering data

The description of the method could be within the activity. A diagram may feature in the answer for example a time related observation schedule within football showing information relevant to the particular aspect selected which was speed and/Cardio Respiratory Endurance. In the answer the candidate may make reference to the process as to how the information was gathered. A narrative account of what was done and **why** should be obvious showing logical thinking. Methods could include video/performance profiles/checklists/stroke counts/breath counts/pulse counts/feedback-reliability and validity of method should be apparent.

Methods could come from out with activity. For example Standardised tests will also be described, these could include:

Physical – 12 minute Cooper test, Sit and reach test, Harvard step test, Bleep test

Skill related – Illinois agility test, Ruler drop, Alternate hand throw.

Mental-Questionnaires or self evaluation tests, internal/external feedback.

(c) **Appropriate methods of training to improve physical ie skill related and mental fitness**

The candidates' responses will depend on the choice of activity, the type or aspect of fitness and phase of training selected. Various methods of training could be chosen and some candidates may choose a one session or a block of time to describe what they did. Training could be within activity/out with ie combination and involve some of the following methods fartlek/continuous/conditioning/ interval/circuit/weight training/relaxation/breathing/ rehearsal.

For example *I used interval training for swimming ….warm up of 8 lengths multi stroke…then some stroke improvement… then main set….6 × 50 metre swim with a minute rest between each set….then sub set….6 × 50….45 sec recovery. This was appropriate because it enables high intensity work combined with rest to allow me to train for a longer period of time and thus gaining greater benefits from training.*

***Training must be linked to the phase selected.***

(d) The candidate should show an understanding of how the training programme has affected their performance. Eg *now that I have increased CRE, as a midfielder I am able to track my opponent more effectively and can now last the whole 90 minutes of the game.*

(e) The candidate should identify a future development need from to further improve their performance. A good response will show how they identified this future development need, what specific difficulties they had and a summary of how they intended to work on this.

4. (a) **Physical fitness** – Cardio Respiratory Endurance; speed; muscular endurance; flexibility; stamina; strength; speed endurance; power.

   **Skill related fitness** – reaction time; agility; co-ordination; balance; timing.

   **Mental fitness** – level of arousal; rehearsal; managing emotion; concentration.

   All responses should suggest how the type or aspect(s) chosen relate to effective performance in the activity.

   **Physical fitness** – eg *in football a high level of Cardio Respiratory Endurance and speed endurance allowed me to track back and help my defence….; as well as support the attackers…; throughout the whole game…; also having good strength as a defender allowed me to jump and challenge for high balls and crosses…; and win tackles against the opposition.*

   **Skill related fitness** – eg *in badminton having good agility will allow me quick movement….; to reach the shuttle or change direction if necessary and return the shuttle to put my opponent under pressure. Good timing will allow me to hit the shuttle at the correct height above me giving me more chance to win a point because my opponent will struggle to return it.*

   **Mental fitness** – eg *in basketball as the ball carrier by managing my emotions I was able to handle the pressure my opponent was putting on me when closely marking…; I was able to make the correct decision and carry out the correct pass to my team mate successfully …; taking a free throw by managing my emotions and rehearsing my routine in my mind I was able to make the free throw successful.*

(b) **Principles of training**

The answer must refer to the principles of training. Most of the following principles should be referred to: specificity to activity; person and performance; progressive overload; frequency; intensity; duration; adaptation; rest/recovery; over training; reversibility.

Candidates will probably have a description of how they were applied to programme and also explanation and justification of why they were considered.

Eg *I made sure the training was specific to the weakness identified…; also demands of activity…; I trained 3 times per week with rest every other …; allowed body to recover …; applied overload after week 3…; increased number of sets …; training became harder and body adapted to new load …; as I was getting fitter…; variety within programme….; prevent boredom and keep motivation high.*

(c) **Appropriate methods of training to improve physical ie skill related and mental fitness**

The candidates' responses will depend on the choice of activity and the aspect of fitness selected. Various methods of training could be chosen and some candidates may choose a one session or a block of time to describe what they did. Training methods could be within activity, out with or combination and involve some of the following methods Fartlek; continuous; conditioning; interval; circuit; weight training; relaxation; breathing; rehearsal.

Eg *I used interval training for swimming…; warm up of 8 lengths multi stroke…; then some stroke improvement…; then main set…; 6 × 50 metre swim with a minute rest between each set…; then sub set….; 6 × 50…; 45 sec recovery…; This was appropriate because it enables high intensity work combined with rest to allow me to train for a longer period of time and thus gaining greater benefits from training.*

(d) **The importance of planning and monitoring training using particular methods**

Methods used could include: video; observation schedules; training diary; logbook; personal evaluation or game/ performance analysis.

(e) **The monitoring process**

A good response will show knowledge about the purpose and importance of the process. It may provide qualitative or quantitative details of whether the training is effective/ working-it can substantiate the specific fitness progress explanations may include – provide evidence to compare progress/targets/improvements — enables changes to be made – ensure future targets-further challenges-promotes motivation – whether training method was appropriate- deciding if training was at correct intensity – whether short term or long term goals had been achieved.

**SKILLS AND TECHNIQUES**

5. (a) **Features of a skilled performance**

A good response may suggest the range and qualities that are evident in a skilled ie model performance.

A link to other relevant factors may include; a repertoire of skills evident and executed at the correct time with consistency, fluency, etc. Movements ie application of skills seem effortless. Management of emotions are controlled. A degree of confidence. Few unforced errors. Makes appropriate decisions when under pressure etc.

(b) **Gathering Information on Performance Strengths or Weaknesses**

A link to identified strengths and or weaknesses may be evident. A good response will include reference to whole performance (initial data) and specific (focussed data). To substantiate claims reference should be made to one or more of the following:

- Movement Analysis (Observation checklist, Match Analysis sheet)
- Mechanical Analysis of force, levers, propulsion etc
- Consideration of Quality: reflecting on whether your skill or technique was controlled/fluent, or fast/slow?
- Video – Comparison of your performance with that of a model performer. The video allowed playback, freeze frame.

(c) **Whole performance development**

The responses offered may suggest the impact of skill/technique in WHOLE performance eg many errors; less points won; less confidence etc.

(d) **Programme of work**

The responses offered will depend on the candidate's choice of skill ie technique identified for development.

The response may include details of the appropriateness of the methods of practice/development programme followed. The programme followed should refer to some of the following considerations: Stages of Learning, skill complexity/skill classification, Model Performer, feedback, goal setting... etc.

Programme references may include details of weeks 1&2, weeks 3&4, weeks 5&6, etc. OR *I used a gradual build up ie whole part whole approach to my development programme.* In this respect the notion of reliability ie validity should be apparent and justified etc.

The content and structure given must be justified with progressions exemplified to demonstrate sound Knowledge and Understanding. For example, *as I was at the cognitive stage — I used many shadow/repetition practices to ensure... etc. At the associative stage I used some shadow/repetition practices.etc. At the automatic stage of learning I knew to use more pressure as this would challenge me more...etc I found the? Skill very difficult so decided to use gradual build up as this would ... etc. In weeks 1&2, I concentrated more on simple drills... in weeks 3-4, I progressed to more complex drills such as .... etc this built my confidence as I reached my target of... etc*
A link to other relevant factors may include; whole part, gradual build up, mass/distributed, closed/open contexts, repetitions, target setting, model performers etc.

(e) **Monitoring and review**

Reference to appropriate data methods to facilitate comparison of improvements. Many candidates will repeat or include some of the previously mentioned comments.

6. (a) **Stages of learning**

A satisfactory response may give appropriate explanations relevant to the stage of learning described. Examples may be included to highlight their understanding in context; this may be generic or linked to a specific skill/technique.

At the cognitive stage a performer will be reliant on a lot of instruction/feedback. The performer is learning about the sub routines of the skill/technique. Success rate/ effectiveness is not refined etc.

At the associative stage, a performer will still be reliant on instruction/feedback but will be developing ability to self evaluate. The performer is more able to link the sub routines of the skill/technique; the execution of the skill is recognisable but the success rate/effectiveness is still not consistent or highly effective etc.

At the automatic stage, a performer will be less reliant on instruction/feedback with an ability to self evaluate and identify weaknesses. The performer is able to link the sub routines of the skill/technique; the execution of the skill is recognisable with control and consistency etc.

A link to other relevant factors may include; progressions possible from one stage to the next, model/skilled performer etc.

(b) **Practice considerations**

A satisfactory response may include details relevant to the selection and appropriateness of the MOST relevant methods of practice, development or training available. Considerations of different methods will be evident in the process. Examples relevant to selected methods will be included highlighting the selections made.

At the cognitive stage – *many shadow or repetition practices were incorporated.*
At the associative stage – *some shadow or repetition practices progressing to combination drills.*
At the automatic stage of learning – *more pressure or problem solving drills were used to advance and challenge learning and performance development.*
A link to other relevant factors may include; whole part, gradual build up, closed/open contexts etc.

(c) **Motivation/Concentration/Feedback**

In this respect the candidate may give a synopsis of how each factor selected impacted upon their learning and/or their application of skill/technique in the overall performance. Merit should be given according to relevance of explanations offered.

**Motivation** – A satisfactory response may include details of being internally/externally motivated to learn or achieve success. Being motivated enables the performer to be: self driven; to listen to instruction and act on it; it helps the performer to be self determined; give of their best; come from behind; respond to immediate problems or competitive challenges; not worry if mistakes are made and re channel focus.

**Concentration** – A satisfactory response may include details of the need to concentrate/focus on instruction or demonstration offered to ensure effective application of skill or technique, promotes progression or adaptation of skill or technique, ensures bad habits are not formed, enables the performer to perform their role and apply their skills appropriately.
In the context of games concentration enables the performer to stick to role related duties etc.

**Feedback** – A response will include details of receiving internal feedback to progress or refine skill/technique; receiving/giving external feedback (visual/verbal/written) to progress/refine skill/technique of self or that of others. Feedback should be positive and immediate to promote confidence and/or success.

(d) **Whole performance development**

The responses offered may suggest the impact of improved skill/technique development to WHOLE performance effectiveness eg a more consistent application; fewer errors; more points won; a positive benefit including greater confidence etc.

The candidate may also include details referencing specific drills or parts of the programme that benefited their performance, eg *I felt that the repetition drills such as... improved my ability to .... etc.*

(e) **Whole performance development**
Responses should include next development need.

## STRUCTURES, STRATEGIES AND COMPOSITIONS

7. (a) **Data collection on role/performance**
Description of the method(s) used must be offered; a diagram may feature to support answer. A range of relevant methods should be selected ie Observation schedule, Coach Feedback, Video. Information relevant to the particular aspects of the Structure, Strategy or Composition should be evident.

(b) Explanations offered about appropriateness may include the following: provides evidence to compare progress; targets; improvements; is a permanent record; can be used time and time again; aids motivation and ensures further challenge and progress; information can be gathered at the beginning/middle and end etc. If video is used reference should be made to pause/rewind facility etc.

(c) The structures, strategies and/or compositional elements that are fundamental to activities.

### Structure and strategy fundamentals
The following may be referred to or listed:
Using space in attack and defence; tempo of play; speed in attack; delay in defence and principles of play (width; depth and mobility).
The importance should be justified and show both acquired and applied knowledge.
Eg *in basketball I wanted to play a fast tempo game......; attack quickly......; so I made sure that on each opportunity we tried to play a fast break ....; to catch the defence out....; score a quick basket ....; create an overload situation ......; before the defence was organised properly.*

### Structure and compositional fundamentals
The following may be referred to or listed:
Design form; developing motifs; using repetition; variation and contrast; using space effectively; using creativity in performance.
The importance should show both acquired and applied knowledge.
Eg *in dance I started with a simple step motif......; took me forwards then back to starting position....; then sideways....; back to starting .....; I established this as a simple core motif.....; then I developed a second core motif....; .this time a jumping pattern.....; then I began to mix and play with both core motifs ......; to add interest to my dance...; gave my dance variety and quality of movement contrasts.*

(d) The responses will depend on the choice of structure, strategy or composition selected. Responses should start with a description of the problem they faced. For example *in basketball we were playing a 2-1-2 zone...opposition had good outside hooters...scored frequently, we were therefore behind at half time.*

(e) Candidates may show evidence of problem solving and decision making to make their performance more effective. The candidate may decide to change structure, strategy or composition completely. For example *in basketball we were playing a 2-1-2 one...opposition had good outside shooters... scored frequently ...we changed to half court man/man defence to stop them...this led to less successful shots as they were under more pressure ...forced them to try and drive to basket They made more mistakes ...scored less baskets as they were poor at driving to basket...we won more turnovers and could attack more.*

Candidates may decide to alter the structure, strategy or composition. For example *in football we played a 4-4-2 formation ....we found when attacking all 4 players in midfield would be up the park....supporting the forwards ...when the attack broke down the opposition often broke quickly....our midfield were slow to get back...our defence was under pressure... we adapted the structure, strategy or composition by having one player....holding in midfield in front of back four ...one midfield supporting strikers...and two in middle to move back and forward as necessary...this led to a more balanced attack and defence and allowed us to prevent the opposition breaking quickly holding midfielder was able to delay attack ....allow others to get back.*

Candidates may also decide to complete a training programme to address weaknesses.

8. (a) **Select a relevant structure, strategy or composition**
The candidate must describe the Structure, Strategy or Composition. Some will also make reference possibly to the role they played as well.
These will include fast break/zones/1-3-1/horse shoe offence in basketball/man/man defence.
Football-4-2-4 ie 4-3-3/3-5-2
Badminton front-back-side-side
Gymnastics particular sequence-routine
Volleyball-rotation
Hockey penalty corner
For example *in tennis I used a serve volley strategy – I would serve fast and hard to opponent-follow my serve – get into net and position quickly-use a volley to win point-from opponents return.*

(b) **The benefits of various systems of play**
Eg *benefits in football a 3-5-2 formation is easier to dominate midfield.....; can cover wide areas of pitch.....; has a variety of attack options linking midfield and forwards*

(c) **The limitations of various systems of play**
Eg Limitations; *defence can be exposed; by long passes; played straight from defence; midfield can be bypassed.*

(d) **Candidate should select two and explain why they were important**
eg
**Using information on team/individual performance to make appropriate decisions when developing, and monitoring performance**
Information may come from before performance. Eg *previous knowledge of weather or playing surface.* It may come from during performance, eg *time and score.* This information would then be used to plan and develop performance by processing this information and then taking decisions to develop performance.

(e) **Monitoring**
It provides evidence to compare progress/targets/ improvements; aids motivation; gives evidence on whether programme of work carried out has been effective; checking whether training methods were appropriate; ensures progress and further development; gives feedback on performance; training at correct intensity; if improvements were made in areas/weaknesses you targeted; making sure not overworking; analyses training on an ongoing basis; provides information to plan adjustments to training.

# INTERMEDIATE 2 PHYSICAL EDUCATION 2012

In relation to **all** questions it should be noted that the relevance of the content in the candidates' responses will depend on:

- the activity selected
- the performance focus
- the training/development programme/programme of work selected
- the practical experiences of their course as the contexts for answers.

## PERFORMANCE APPRECIATION

1. (a) **Qualities**

   In relation to any of the qualities selected a description should be offered of a quality or qualities which were strengths in the candidate's performance.

   Candidates may demonstrate acquired Knowledge and Understanding in respect of their performance strengths.

   **Technical Qualities:** Reference may be made to a repertoire of skills, eg *dribbling, passing, shooting, etc is consistent and accurate.* This may be accompanied by clarification of success rate or quality of execution or PAR. Reference may also be made to the classification of skills demanded, eg simple/complex etc.

   **Physical Qualities:** Reference may be made to more than one aspect of fitness. To support acquired or applied Knowledge and Understanding the candidate must describe how the selected aspect of fitness was a strength within their quality performance.

   eg *high levels of Cardio Respiratory Endurance, Speed Endurance helped maintain pace and track my opponents continuously…*

   **Personal Qualities:** Reference may be made to inherent qualities, eg *qualities such as being determined or confident or competitive, etc helped because opponents felt threatened…*

   **Special Qualities:** Reference may be made to the ability to create opportunity, deceive opponents, make performance look more dynamic, apply flair, had the ability to choreograph routines, link skills, etc.

   For example, *These unique qualities helped to fake intent and so wrong-foot opponents. The routine was exciting to watch. This helped gain more points etc.*

   The strengths of their performance must be linked to one or more of the qualities listed above. Candidates may also go down the demands route as the word 'demands' is in the question.

   (b) **Qualities**

   In relation to any of the qualities selected a description should be offered of a quality or qualities which were a weakness to the candidate's performance.

   Candidates may demonstrate acquired Knowledge and Understanding in respect of their performance weaknesses.

   **Technical Qualities:** Reference may be made to a repertoire of skills, eg *dribbling, passing, shooting, etc is not consistent or accurate.* This may be accompanied by clarification of failure rate or quality of execution or PAR. Reference may also be made to the classification of skills demanded, eg simple/complex etc.

   **Physical Qualities:** Reference may be made to more than one aspect of fitness. To support acquired or applied Knowledge and Understanding the candidate must describe how the selected aspect of fitness was a weakness to their performance, eg *poor levels of Cardio Respiratory Endurance meant that I was unable to last the whole length of the games,*

*Speed Endurance unable to maintain pace and track my opponents continuously…*

**Personal Qualities:** Reference may be made to inherent qualities, eg *qualities such as not being determined or confident or competitive… , eg the effects of lack of focus, meant that I missed important shots which would have easily given me the lead.*

**Special Qualities:** Reference may be made to the **inability** to create opportunity, deceive opponents, make performance look more dynamic, apply flair, had the ability to choreograph routines, link skills…etc.

The weaknesses of performance must be linked to one or more of the qualities listed above. Candidates may also go down the demands route as the word 'demands' is in the question.

(c) **Benefits of setting goals and examples of setting goals**

A good response will suggest the importance of establishing short term goals to help reach longer term goals. Examples should be offered to show understanding about performance gains as a result of setting realistic/attainable goals. eg *By setting goals I was able to track whether I was making improvements or not and then make appropriate changes to my training programme. It also helped with my motivation levels, as when I felt I had reached a specific goal it gave me the desire to try to improve even further.*

A response will give examples of specific goals set. For example, *I decided to set myself a short term goal of increasing my power. My long term goal would be to use this effectively when spiking in Volleyball.*

(d) **Course of action**

Candidates must describe a relevant training programme related to their goals. Depending on the type of training programme used the candidate will describe an appropriate training programme. For CRE the candidate may use an interval training programme for swimming. For example, *warm up of 8 lengths multi stroke…; then some stroke improvement…; then main set…; 6 × 50 metre swim with a minute rest between each set…; then sub set…; 6 × 50, 45 sec recovery.*

The candidate would next explain the length of the training, what days they trained on, the duration of the training session, how they measured the intensity of the training. Progressive overload should also be evident within the response, to show that the training becomes more challenging.

(e) **Course effectiveness/impact on performance development**

A good response MUST include evaluative comments and offer examples on how and why candidates thought the course of action taken was effective. The candidate could state what the impact of skill/technique development to WHOLE performance development was. Depending on the type of training programme used the candidate will explain the effects the training had on their performance. For exampe, *After completing my skill development programme to improve my back walk over in Gymnastics, I am now able to use this complex skill to link two skills together smoothly. I am now able to fluently perform a back walkover, which will help me gain more marks for my routine.*

2. (a) **Nature and Demands**

The candidates response should include some of the nature and demands as outlined below. The response must be linked to a specific activity.

**Nature:** Individual/team. The duration of the game/event. The number of player(s)/performers involved. A spectator/audience event. Indoor/outdoor. Directly/indirectly competitive. Objective/subjective scoring systems in application. Codes of conduct.

**Challenges:** Technical, Physical, Mental and Special. Candidates may demonstrate acquired Knowledge and Understanding across all related demands or focus on one more comprehensively. Similarly, candidates may demonstrate acquired Knowledge and Understanding in respect of the unique game/event challenges or emphasise the challenges unique to the role/solo/duo performance relative to the activity selected.

**Special Performance Qualities**

The responses will be wide ranging and relevant to the activity selected. Candidates may demonstrate acquired Knowledge and Understanding in respect of the specific role/solo related demands necessary for an effective performance.

(b) **Gathering information on performance strengths or weaknesses**

Detailed description should be made in one of the following:

- Movement Analysis (Observation checklist, Match Analysis sheet).
- Preparation/Action/Recovery:
- Scatter Diagram, eg *I used a scatter diagram, which is when an observer notes down on a diagram of a badminton court where my shots were played during a game of badminton. My observer would use a notation key to pinpoint exactly where/when my shots were a strength in my game and where/when my shots were a weakness in my game. If, for example I played a successful Overhead clear, it would be noted as OHC√ on the back tramlines of my badminton court diagram. When I completed this scatter diagram, I played an opponent of similar ability to me and we played a game to 15. A third person then completed the scatter diagram as we played.*
- Mechanical Analysis of force, levers, propulsion etc
- Consideration of Quality: reflecting on whether your skill or technique was controlled/fluent, or fast/slow?
- Video – Comparison of your performance with that of a model performer. The video allowed playback, freeze frame.
- Questionnaire: Questions should be relevant to and have responses such as 'done well', 'needs improvement' or mark your performance on a graded scale.

(c) **Mental factors**

Candidates may demonstrate acquired Knowledge and Understanding in their ability to manage emotions. They may describe how they handled stress levels through careful preparation which focuses then into the positive aspects of their performance. They may use a form of mental rehearsal to manage pre performance nerves. Examples of these will be given in the response.

(d) **Mental factors**

Candidates will give an example(s) of how they were unable to manage their emotions successfully. eg - *During my Football performance I felt the defence in our team were not playing to the best of their ability, which led me to become very frustrated. I began to shout to them to cover the ball more, which led me to lose focus on my own role within our team.*

(e) Candidates should select one or more of the methods and describe how they used them – eg, *I used visualisation by imaging my gymnastic sequence and how I could perform it to my best ability. I made sure I performed my routine through in my mind, highlighting the specific links in my performance. Before I began my routine I used a deep breathing technique, of slowly taking three deep breaths, before I started my routine.*

**PREPARATION OF THE BODY**

3. (a) **Physical fitness** – eg, *in badminton CRE is needed to last long rallies and keep my skill level high the whole time...; Speed and strength are important to give power so that the smash is difficult to return.*

**Skill related fitness** – eg, *in badminton having good agility will allow me quick movement...; to reach the shuttle or change direction if necessary and return the shuttle to put my opponent under pressure – also...; good timing will allow me to hit the shuttle at the correct place, giving me more chance to win a point because my opponent struggles to return it.*

**Mental fitness** – eg, *in badminton I need to be able to concentrate for the whole match...; concentrate on each shot...; being focussed...; be determined to win...; not being distracted etc.*

More than one aspect is required to get full marks.

(b) **Physical fitness** – eg, *in football I found it difficult to pass accurately towards the end of the game as I was tired...I also found it difficult to hold the ball up for supporting players as I lacked strength... I also lacked speed which affected my ability to stay close to my opposing player when they played the ball past me*

**Skill related fitness** – eg, *in football I found it difficult to change direction quickly when reacting to a loose ball...I also found it difficult to link skills together losing control of the ball as I attempted to take it down on my chest and then release a pass...I also found it difficult to time my passes where the ball was intercepted as I waited too long*

**Mental-fitness** – eg, *I reacted aggressively when the referee made an incorrect decision...I also got nervous when defending a lead towards the end of the game...I also found it difficult to motivate myself when my team were losing.*

(c) **Principles of training**

You may have a description of how the principles were applied to the programme. For example, *I made sure the training was specific to the weakness identified...also demands of activity...I trained three times per week with rest every other day...I applied overload after week 3...increased number of sets...as I was getting fitter...variety within programme...prevent boredom and keep motivation high...each session lasted 50mins...* Although the question does not ask for a reason why each principle was used, credit will be given if a candidate extends their knowledge.

(d) **The monitoring process**

Responses should consider a description of the different methods that were used to monitor...eg, *I used the leger test to check if I was improving... I used knowledge of results where I checked for improvements... I recorded my results in a training diary which gave an opportunity to check my progress...*

The candidates should describe the monitoring method and the process of how they used their selected method(s), in detail.

(e) **Progressive overload**

Candidates may choose to use the detail from part (c). There should be some demonstration of what the changes were as the programme progressed over time.

For example, *I increased how many days I trained per week. I now trained 3 days a week instead of 2.* **or** *I increased the intensity of the practice by adding another rep to each set during interval training.* **or** *I trained for longer each session, 30 minutes to 40 minutes.* **or** *I reduced the amount of rest I had during practices.*

**4.** (*a*) (i) **Strength**

*Speed was a strength in basketball…when defending I was able to move across the surface area quickly to put pressure on my opposing player…I could also drive past players whilst dribbling giving me space and time…*

*Agility was a strength in badminton…I could lunge down low to return net shots…I could also change direction quickly as the shuttle was played over my head to the back of the court.*

(ii) **Weakness**

*CVE was a weakness in hockey…I found it difficult to maintain my accuracy when shooting as I was tired towards the end of the game…I also found it difficult to recover from supporting runs near the end of the game…*

*I lacked strength during my gymnastics sequence…I found it difficult to take my weight on my hands whilst doing a handstand…My lack of strength also prevented me from holding my shoulder stand for the required time…*

(*b*) **Accurate collection and recording of data**

**Gathering data:** The description of the method could be within the activity. A diagram may feature in the answer for example a time related observation schedule within football showing information relevant to the particular aspect selected, which was speed and/Cardio Respiratory Endurance. In the answer the candidate may make reference to the process as to how the information was gathered. A narrative account of what was done. Methods could include video/performance profiles/checklists/stroke counts/breath counts/pulse counts/feedback – reliability and validity of method could be apparent. Methods could come from outwith the activity. For example, standardised tests could also be described and these could include:

Physical – 12 minute Cooper test, Sit and reach test, Harvard step test, Bleep test

Skill related – Illinois agility test, Ruler drop, Alternate hand throw

Mental – Questionnaires or self evaluation tests, internal/external feedback.

**Why test was useful**

- I was able to compare against national norms
- Nationally recognised tests adding to validity
- I could you use the test to set targets, giving me something to work towards
- I could use the test to compare previous result to check for improvements

(*c*) Candidates may choose to select from a range of factors, the question is open in nature eg,…*I considered how many days a week I trained… I trained 3 days…I consider how long my programme should last…I choose 6 weeks…I considered the methods of training I should use…I used fartlek and conditioning training…I considered when I should test…I decided in weeks 1, 3 and 5…I considered which methods I should use to monitor…I used heart rate watches and knowledge of results.*

(*d*) **Appropriate methods of training to improve physical/skill related and mental fitness**

The candidates' responses will depend on the choice of activity, the aspect of fitness selected. Various methods of training could be chosen and some candidates may choose a one session or a block of time to describe what they did. Training methods could be within activity, outwith or combination and involve some of the following methods – fartlek, continuous, conditioning, interval, circuit, weight training, relaxation, breathing, rehearsal.

For example, *I used interval training for swimming…; .warm up of 8 lengths multi stroke…; then some stroke improvement…; then main set…; 6 × 50 metre swim with a minute rest between each set…; then sub set…; 6 × 50…; 45 sec recovery…*

(*e*) **Appropriate methods of training to improve physical/skill related and mental fitness**

eg, *Interval Training… this was appropriate because it enables high intensity work combined with rest to allow me to train for a longer period of time and thus gaining greater benefits from training.*

*Fartlek…this was appropriate as the method mirrored the movements that I would use in a game of football…it was also easy to monitor allowing me to make changes at the correct time…I was also motivated to beat the number of laps I did during the training…*

**SKILLS AND TECHNIQUES**

**5.** (*a*) **Gathering data**

- Movement Analysis (Observation checklist, Match Analysis sheet, Pre/Action/Recovery)
- Mechanical Analysis of force, levers, propulsion etc Scatter Diagram eg, *I used a scatter diagram, which is when an observer notes down on a diagram of a Badminton court where my shots were played during a game of badminton. My observer would use a notation key to pinpoint exactly where/when my shots were a strength in my game and where/when my shots were a weakness in my game. If, for example I played a successful Overhead clear, it would be noted as OHC√ on the back tramlines of my badminton court diagram. When I completed this scatter diagram, I played an opponent of similar ability to me and we played a game to 15. A third person then completed the scatter diagram as we played.*
- Consideration of Quality: reflecting on whether your skill or technique was controlled/fluent, or fast/slow.
- Video – Comparison of your performance with that of a model performer. The video allowed playback, freeze frame.
- Initial Data/Match Analysis
- Scatter Diagram
- Skill Test

(*b*) **Effect of strong skill on performance**

Candidates will select a skill within their activity which was a strength. For example, *During my basketball game dribbling was a strength within my game. This allowed me to dribble past defenders using both my right and left hand with control. I was also able to use my dribbling skills during our attack, where I was able to dribble down the court at speed.*

(*c*) **Effect of weak skill on performance**

Candidates will select a skill within their activity which was a weakness. For example, *During my basketball game my lay-up was a weakness within my game. I was unable to drive into space within the key to perform a lay-up successfully. The ball was always stolen from me or I used too many steps. I often missed easy shots which led to my team being behind in the game.*

(*d*) **Programme of work**

The responses offered will depend on the candidate's choice of skill/technique identified for development.

The programme followed should refer to some of the following considerations: stages of learning, length of training programme, training methods used, work to rest ratio, progression, goals

Programme references may include details of weeks 1&2, weeks 3&4, weeks 5&6, etc. **or** *I used a gradual build up/whole part whole approach to my development programme.*

The content and structure given must be justified with progressions exemplified to demonstrate sound Knowledge and Understanding. For example, *As I was at the cognitive stage – I used many shadow/repetition practices to ensure… etc. At the associative stage I used some shadow/repetition practices etc. At the automatic stage of learning I knew to use more pressure as this would challenge me more…etc. I found the skill… very difficult so decided to use gradual build up as this would … etc. In weeks 1 & 2, I concentrated more on simple drills… in weeks 3 – 4; I progressed to more complex drills such as …. etc. This built my confidence as I reached my target of… etc.*

(e) **Feedback**

Some responses may include;

- Positive
- Negative
- Continuous
- internal/external feedback
- visual
- verbal
- written

All should be related to the actual performance and the activity selected. For example, *as I was in the cognitive stage of learning I relied heavily on external feedback from my coach. When I was in a practice situation he gave me verbal feedback constantly as I played my overhead clear. On occasions he also demonstrated specific parts of the skill that he felt I could improve upon.*

6. (a) **Methods of Practice**

A good response may include details relevant to the selection and appropriateness of the MOST relevant methods of practice, development or training available. Considerations of different methods will be evident in the process. Examples relevant to selected methods will be included, highlighting the selections made.

At the cognitive stage – *I used a shadow practice where I copied the movement of my skill without the pressure of a shuttle cock. eg I carefully copied the movements required for a Backhand clear, taking it step by step. The preparation stage, the movement to the shuttle and then the actual contact position. I worked for about 3 mins, rested then completed again.*

At the automatic stage of learning – *more pressure or problem solving drills were used. eg I had to perform a Backhand clear and then move quickly to the net to perform a net shot. My partner would then place the shuttle cock high to my Backhand. I had to move quickly and efficiently to the back to play a successful Backhand clear.*

(b) **Principles of effective practice**

For example, practice should be specific, measurable, attainable, realistic, time related, exciting and regular…*as my programme was specific it helped me to achieve success…I could target the specific part of my technique that need most improvement…I knew to set targets and raise them once…this ensures my practice was motivating etc.*

Other relevant knowledge will reference factors such as practice needs to show progression to ensure targets were reached. Increased motivation, improved confidence, consideration of work rest ratio etc.

(c) **Motivation**

- Internal and/or external motivation. The candidate should explain how they used their own motivational levels or the motivation of others to help them within their programme. eg they may be determined to respond to challenges within their training and to successfully improve within training.

  They can channel their thoughts to consistently trying to improve. They are consistently being motivated to win/improve.

**Concentration**

- To make sure bad habits are not learnt when completing their training. They must be able to concentrate on methods used within their training programme and complete them correctly. They must also be able to concentrate on any feedback given during their training programme.
- In games player being able to stick to their role and read situations/make decisions

**Feedback**

- Should be positive, immediate during their training programme. External feedback may be used when in the cognitive stage of learning, so that the skill is being learnt properly. Internal feedback may be used during training when repeating the action so the performer can feel how the skill is performed successfully.
- Candidate may also refer to visual/verbal/written types of feedback and how they used this within their training.

(d) **The importance of monitoring and reviewing**

- Evaluating performance will lead to comparison of any improvements made, this will be highlighted at the end of the programme.
- See whether targets set have been achieved or not
- Gaining and acting on feedback which may have been received during training.
- Aids motivation – if a definite improvement has been made by the end of the programme, the performer becomes more motivated to improve further.
- Ensures further challenge and progress, when planning the next steps.

(e) **Whole performance development**

The responses offered may suggest the impact of improved skill/technique programme to WHOLE performance effectiveness, eg a more consistent application; fewer errors; more points won; a positive benefit including greater confidence etc.

The candidate may also include details referencing specific drills or parts of the programme that benefited their performance, eg, *I felt that the repetition drills such as repeating my overhead clear, allowed me to practice my transfer of weight, which helped me improve my ability to generate more power in my shot. This helped me to clear the shuttlecock to the back court, placing my opponent under pressure.*

## STRUCTURES, STRATEGIES AND COMPOSITIONS

7. (a) **Select a relevant structure, strategy or composition**

The candidate must describe their role within Structure, Strategy or Composition. Some may do this by describing the whole strategy and referring to the role that they played as they describe the whole strategy. Alternatively some may describe their role in isolation having identified the Structure, Strategy or Composition.

These will include fast break/zones/1-3-1/horse shoe offence in basketball/man/man defence.

Football-4-2-4 ie 4-3-3/3-5-2

Badminton front-back-side-side

Gymnastics particular sequence-routine

Volleyball-rotation

Hockey penalty corner

For example, fast break…*I played the guard in the strategy…I called the code and broke wide to the elbow of the key…I received a pass in both hands…I dribbled quickly up the middle lane with the ball under control…I assessed my options at the top of the key…I made a quick decision and made a pass to the forward who was in most space…*

4-4-2... *I played as a right winger in midfield...in attack I had to be disciplined and stay on the touchline to create width...on receiving the ball I had to make a decision of how I was going to beat my full back to get a cross into the box...I used my speed to knock it passed and ran to the touchline where I would play a range of crosses depending who was offering support in the box...whilst defending I had to back track quickly to offer support to the full back who was on my side...*

(b) **Roles and relationships**

Individual strengths in a structure, strategy or composition. For example... *I played as a centre in the 2.1.2 Zone defence as I was tall...this allowed me to form a rebounding triangle with the baseline players...my height meant that I could jump early to win the ball gaining possession for my team...I was also strong...this 'boxed' out opposing players who were attempting to contest the rebounds...I also was fast across the surface area...this allowed me to provide cover if the seams of the zone were broken...*

For example... *I played as a centre forward in hockey...my speed allowed me to stretch the opposition's defence leaving a larger area for the supporting players to exploit...I was also quick to throw passes giving me time and space to make more effective decisions...I could also link up effectively with the midfield players ...*

(c) **The limitations of various systems of play**

The responses may refer to the structure, strategy or composition in a general way
For example, 4.4.2 in football... *having only two attacking made our attack less threating...also only having four players in defence meant that we were often left without cover if a long ball was played over the top.*
Alternatively...responses may link directly to problems with a specific player/role/performance...
Hockey, short corner...*the person hitting the ball failed to hit it quickly enough across the area...this allowed the defending players to put pressure on the hitting player more quickly...the person stopping the ball was often under too much pressure due to the ball being under hit...they often took their eye off the ball as they saw the oncoming defenders advancing on them...*

(d) They may show evidence of problem solving and decision making to make their performance more effective. The candidate may decide to change structure, strategy or composition completely. For example, *in basketball we were playing a 2-1-2 zone... opposition had good outside shooters...scored frequently ...we changed to half court man/man defence to stop them...this led to less successful shots as they were under more pressure ...forced them to try and drive to basket. They made more mistakes ...scored fewer baskets as they were poor at driving to basket...we won more turnovers and could attack more.*

The candidate may decide to adapt the structure, strategy or composition. For example, *in football we played a 4-4-2 formation ...we found when attacking all 4 players in midfield would be up the park....supporting the forwards ...when the attack broke down the opposition often broke quickly....our midfield were slow to get back...our defence was under pressure...we adapted the structure, strategy or composition by having one player....holding in midfield in front of back four ...one midfield player supporting strikers...and two in middle to move back and forward as necessary...this led to a more balanced attack and defence and allowed us to prevent the opposition breaking quickly ...holding midfielder was able to delay attack ...allow others to get back.*

The candidate may also decide to complete a training programme to address weaknesses. This may demonstrate a range of progressive practices/drills linked specifically to the weak areas identified in part (c).

(e) The question is open in nature. Candidates should identify areas and then go on to provide reasons why it would further develop performance.

For example, *in volleyball...we could aim to further improve our timing when jumping to block...this would put the opposing attack under more pressure allowing us to defend more effectively picking the ball up on more occasions...*

In basketball... *the guard could aim to improve their timing of the pass at the top of the key...this would further improve the strategy as the forwards could drive in under less pressure to attempt a lay...scoring more points.*

8. (a) **Select a relevant structure, strategy or composition**
The candidate must describe the Structure, Strategy or Composition. These will include fast break/zones/1-3-1/horse shoe offence in basketball/man/man defence.
Football: 4-2-4/4-3-3/3-5-2
Badminton front-back-side-side
Gymnastics particular sequence-routine
Volleyball – rotation
Hockey – penalty corner

The description should include details regarding the specific roles within the strategy and what each player did within their role.

Fast Break: *The strategy consists of 5 players; two centres, two forwards and a point guard...centre wins rebound...guard calls code and breaks to elbow of the key...centre pivots and passes accurately to guard...forwards sprint forward filling right and left lanes...guard dribbles quickly up the centre of the court...*

(b) Candidates may respond to the question in two ways. Firstly they may provide an applied knowledge response where the give reasons on the benefits of the strategy eg,

Fast break...*it leaves the opponent's defence stretched across a large surface area giving our team more space to exploit...the forwards width at the top of the key stretched the opposition's defence giving the guard more space to execute the final pass at the top of the key*
Alternatively the candidate may answer through strengths in their selected strategy...
3-5-2 in football...*we had fast wing backs who were able to support the forwards...they were disciplined and provided width to the attack...our three defenders were strong and tall and the opposing strikers found it difficult to hold up the ball due to our defenders being more physical.*

(c) The candidates may attempt the question through using their applied knowledge or identifying performance weaknesses.

For example, in Netball – *during our centre pass strategy we found that the first two options were not available due to our players being double marked, as our opponents had worked out the pattern of our centre pass strategy. Our team panicked and were unable to complete the series of passes.*

(d) **Changing/ adapting a structure, strategy or composition in response to performance demands**
The responses will depend on the choice of structure, strategy or composition selected. For example, in basketball – *we were playing a 2-1-2 zone...opposition had good outside shooters... scored frequently. We adapted the zone strategy to a box +1 to put pressure on the outside shooter.*

The candidate may decide to alter the structure, strategy or composition.
For example, *in football we played a 4-4-2 formation...we found when attacking...all 4 players in midfield would be up the park...supporting the forwards...when the attack broke*

*down the opposition often broke quickly…our midfield were slow to get back…our defence was under pressure…We changed to a 3-5-2…this gave us the option of having a sitting midfielder who positioned themselves in front of the defence as we attacked…as our attack broke down the sitting midfielder could pressure the ball delaying the attack giving the supporting midfielders a chance to recover…*

(e) **Affect on whole performance**

The response should provide details regarding the improvement to whole performance.

2.1. 2 zone to sagging man to man…*players now responsible for marking own player…putting more pressure on attack…lead to more turnovers…confidence grew as we prevented the opposition scoring…less space for the opposing team to exploit space in key as 'help' defence was available…fewer baskets conceded…*

Hey! I've done it

**i BrightRED** PUBLISHING

© 2012 SQA/Bright Red Publishing Ltd, All Rights Reserved

Published by Bright Red Publishing Ltd, 6 Stafford Street, Edinburgh, EH3 7AU
Tel: 0131 220 5804, Fax: 0131 220 6710, enquiries: sales@brightredpublishing.co.uk,
www.brightredpublishing.co.uk

Official SQA answers to 978-1-84948-278-3
2008-2012